Dedication

To our political warriors who will save our nation from tyranny—those who will enable our posterity to have a future of freedom and Liberty.

Table of Contents

Introduction

"Those who cannot remember the past, are condemned to repeat it."
George Santayana, 1905

Let's paraphrase Santayana's words: If you *refuse* to learn history, you're doomed to repeat it. However, if you learn from history, you won't repeat it.

The word "refuse" is emphasized because our schools no longer teach American history as it should be taught. The school system, which is controlled by government and politicians, refuses to teach our true history...the history of the magnificence of the Declaration of Independence and the Constitution. No other nation in the world has come close to duplicating those documents which proclaim Liberty for our citizens. None! The promises made in those two documents are the reasons that so many people have immigrated to this country. They sought and wanted the freedom and liberty which they promise.

The world is run by ideas. Some are good, some are bad. This isn't rocket science—it's a fact of life. You're going to be studying some of the ideas which have propelled the United States and the rest of the world into conflict. There are ideas derived from the Judeo-Christian ethic, and there are ideas that oppose this ethic. It's as simple as that—good versus evil.

The main thrust of this effort is to piece together American historical political events of the past one hundred years to show you how socialism and/or communism has taken root in our government. A great deal of the historical information used in this dissertation comes from easily accessible online sources such as *Wikipedia*.

Let's start with the objectives of Karl Marx as stated in his Communist Manifesto in 1848, then we'll touch on the takeover of a government using the revolutionary method, i.e., the violent Bolshevik Revolution in Russia in 1917. Following that, we'll review the nonviolent legislative approach as was done by the Czechoslovakian Communist Party in 1946.

From Czechoslovakia, we shall come back to the United States and go to the administration of Woodrow Wilson to learn a little of what took place when he was president. Generally speaking, he was the catalyst that started our national decline from freedom and liberty into the dark oppression of socialism. He was also a strong proponent of a one-world government, with the League of Nations being one of his pet projects.

We'll examine the American Civil Liberties Union (ACLU) and its founders' principles.

We shall take a look at the beginning of the Council on Foreign Relations (CFR), which was established at about the same time as the ACLU.

A short excursion into the first congressional hearings on communism in the United States will be made.

We'll also review some of the basics of Saul Alinsky's *Rules for Radicals.* That will bring up the hair on the back of your neck. To me, it's the final piece of the puzzle that leads us to the White House and the philosophy (modus operandi) of its current tenant.

You'll be amazed to learn the ACLU, the CFR, and the initial Senate hearings on communism in the U. S. all started in 1920 give or take a year or two. This all occurred at the end of Wilson's second term in office.

Before we go too far afield, let's review some of George Washington's comments to his cabinet in his first farewell address of September 17, 1796. Keep them in mind as you study the rest of the book. The following material came from an online source known as *Archiving Early America* at www.earlyamerica.com. Emphasis is mine in the ensuing quotation:

> The unity of Government, which constitutes you one people, is also now dear to you. It is justly so; for it is a main pillar in the edifice of your real independence, the support of your tranquillity at home, your peace abroad; of your safety; of your prosperity; of that very Liberty, which you so highly prize. *But as it is easy to foresee, that, from different causes and from different quarters, much pains will be taken, many artifices employed, to weaken in your minds the conviction of this truth; as this is the point in your political fortress against which the batteries of internal and external enemies will be most constantly and actively (though often covertly and insidiously) directed, it is of infinite moment, that you should properly estimate the immense value of your national Union to your collective and individual happiness;* that you should cherish a cordial, habitual, and immovable attachment to it; accustoming yourselves to think and

speak of it as of the Palladium of your political safety and prosperity; watching for its preservation with jealous anxiety; discountenancing whatever may suggest even a suspicion, that it can in any event be abandoned; and indignantly frowning upon the first dawning of every attempt to alienate any portion of our country from the rest, or to enfeeble the sacred ties which now link together the various parts...

Towards the preservation of your government, and the permanency of your present happy state, it is requisite, not only that you steadily discountenance irregular oppositions to its acknowledged authority, but also that you resist with care the spirit of innovation upon its principles, however specious the pretexts. One method of assault may be to effect, in the forms of the constitution, alterations, which will impair the energy of the system, and thus to undermine what cannot be directly overthrown...

Of all the dispositions and habits, which lead to political prosperity, Religion and Morality are indispensable supports. In vain would that man claim the tribute of Patriotism, who should labor to subvert these great pillars of human happiness, these firmest props of the duties of Men and Citizens. The mere Politician, equally with the pious man, ought to respect and to cherish them. A volume could not trace all their connexions with private and public felicity. Let it simply be asked, Where is the security for property, for reputation, for life, if the sense of religious obligation desert the oaths, which are the instruments of investigation in Courts of Justice? *And let us with caution indulge the supposition, that morality can be maintained without religion. Whatever may be conceded to the influence of refined education on minds of peculiar structure, reason and experience both forbid us to expect, that national morality can prevail in exclusion of religious principle.*

It is substantially true that virtue or morality is a necessary well-spring of popular government. The rule, indeed, extends with more or less force to every species of free government. Who, that is a sincere friend to it, can look with indifference upon attempts to shake the foundation of the fabric?

3

When you consider Washington's words in the context of the history of the United States during the past one hundred years, you must agree that he was gifted with a great prescience.

Since Marxism has been so influential in the U. S. during the past one hundred years, let's study...

Karl's objectives

In 1848, only fifty-one years later, Karl Marx completed his *Communist Manifesto*. He had ten objectives that he hoped to achieve. They were:
1. Abolition of property in land and application of all rents of land to public purposes.
2. A heavy progressive or graduated income tax.
3. Abolition of all right of inheritance.
4. Confiscation of the property of all emigrants and rebels.
5. Centralisation of credit in the hands of the State, by means of a national bank with State capital and an exclusive monopoly.
6. Centralisation of the means of communication and transport in the hands of the State.
7. Extension of factories and instruments of production owned by the State; the bringing into cultivation of waste-lands, and the improvement of the soil generally in accordance with a common plan.
8. Equal liability of all to labour. Establishment of industrial armies, especially for agriculture.
9. Combination of agriculture with manufacturing industries; gradual abolition of the distinction between town and country, by a more equitable distribution of the population over the country.
10. Free education for all children in public schools. Abolition of children's factory labour in its present form and combination of education with industrial production.

The above data was found in the *Wikipedia* explanation of the document. I reviewed other sources to see if the wording of the objectives was the same and it was. Therefore, I'm confident of the accuracy of the material.

Let's review some of the events that lead me to believe we're almost a failed capitalist republic that's being replaced by a socialist nation.

Item 1. **The abolition of property rights**. The Kelo vs City of New London case in 2005 was a good example of government effort to abuse the property rights of the individual as protected under Section 1 of the XIVth Amendment to the Constitution.

The plaintiff, Kelo, won the case, but with great gnashing of teeth and tearing of hair, so to speak. The case, which was about eminent domain, went all the way to the U. S. Supreme Court, and was decided in behalf of the plaintiff by a 5-4 margin, which was divided along politically ideological lines.

Essentially, the City of New London, CT wanted to take Kelo's home and use the property for a proprietary pursuit that would have generated a greater tax revenue by the economic development of the ground. Eventually, the project was abandoned because funding could not be found. The land became a dump for the city.

Item 2. **The progressive income tax** was implemented during Woodrow Wilson's first administration in 1913 as the 16th Amendment to the Constitution. Wilson was a Democrat. As originally framed, the tax started at 1% and escalated to a maximum of 7%. *Wikipedia—the Revenue Act of 1913.*

Item 3. The **abolition of all rights of inheritance** came about in 1916, also under Woodrow Wilson (D). It was known as the Federal & State Estate Tax. This law reformed probate laws and limited inheritance by way of arbitrary inheritance tax statutes.

Item 4. **The confiscation of the property** of all emigrants and rebels is done through government seizures, tax liens and Executive Order by the President. This was done by Executive Order 11490 [President Richard M. Nixon (R)], which gives private land to the Department of Urban Development, and the imprisonment of terrorists (good idea) and those who speak out or write against the government (an infringement of freedom of speech. Not a good idea. It's unconstitutional.).

Item 5. **The centralization of credit in the hands of the state**, by means of a national bank with State capital and an exclusive monopoly. We call this the Federal Reserve Act, which was passed in 1913 under the Wilson administration. This is the legislation that established the Federal Reserve banking system.

5

6. **The centralization of the means of communications and transportation in the hands of the State.** This was achieved by the establishment of the Federal Communications Commission [1934 under Franklin Delano Roosevelt (D.)], the Interstate Commerce Commission [1887 under Grover Cleveland (D)], and the Department of Transportation [1966 under Lyndon B. Johnson (D)].

7. **State-owned factories and instruments of production** exist indirectly under our current government through The Desert Land Act and the Department of Agriculture and the various industrial bailouts that have taken place during the past few years. General Motors and Chrysler immediately come to mind.

Other departments of government that add to the control and regulation of commerce are the Department of Commerce and Labor; the Department of the Interior; the Environmental Protection Agency; the Bureau of Land Management; the Bureau of Reclamation; the Bureau of Mines; the National Park Service; and the IRS.

8. The equal liability of all to labor and the **establishment of industrial and agricultural armies** could be interpreted to mean the growth of the labor movement. Our government seems to be run by the labor unions that can do no wrong. Unions provide strong financial support for Democrat candidates at any level of government, and are indispensable to a socialist government.

9. Marx's dream of the combination of the agricultural and manufacturing industries accompanied by the **gradual abolition between country and town** seems to be taking place as a normal course of demographic change. We've seen the population move from the agrarian to the industrial as a natural phenomenon. Marx wanted the change to be achieved by government-controlled equal distribution of population.

As the demographics have changed, and our cities have become more and more heavily populated by legal and illegal immigrants, we're seeing a very strong trend to the Marxist ideology. There is a strong case to be made that this trend is supported by progressive ideologues in our union-controlled education system that is controlled by a union-dominated government.

10. Marx's call for **free education for all children in public schools,** abolition of child labor, and the combination of education with industrial

production was something of a pipe dream until governments throughout the world began to take control of the education system.

 By doing so, governments can control what is taught and how it's taught to the students. This is the sauce from which tyranny is made by the use of the school as a means of subliminal indoctrination.

 There are many dictators today, and from the past, who understand and understood the importance of controlling the minds of the children. During the past one hundred years, those who followed the premise to good advantage were Vladimir Lenin (leader of the Russian Bolshevik Revolution), Joseph Stalin (Soviet dictator who was among the Bolshevik revolutionaries who brought about the October Revolution in Russia in 1917 and later held the position of General Secretary of the Communist Party of the Soviet Union's Central Committee from 1922 until his death in 1953.), Hirohito (emperor of Japan in World War II), and Adolph Hitler, leader of the National Socialist German Workers Party (German: Nationalsozialistische Deutsche Arbeiterpartei, (NSDAP), commonly referred to as the Nazi Party). He was chancellor of Germany from 1933 to 1945 and dictator of Nazi Germany (as Führer und Reichskanzler) from 1934 to 1945.

 As you consider the foregoing facts and hypotheses, one must wonder if the United States has become a socialist nation.

And now on to...

The Russian Bolshevik Revolution of 1917

 After many years of rule by nobility, namely the Romanov family, a series of revolutions began taking place in Russia. The first was in 1905. There were worker strikes, "restlessness" among the peasants, and military mutinies. All of this led to the establishment of a limited constitutional monarchy under Tsar Nicholas II, the State Duma of the Russian Empire, the multi-party system, and the Russian Constitution of 1906. (A historical footnote...Tsar Nicholas II of the Romanov family was the last emperor of Russia.)

After the overthrow of the czarist government of the Romanovs in February, 1917, a quasi-republican provisional government led by Alexander Kerensky was established in May, 1917. Kerensky promoted freedom of speech, released thousands of political prisoners, and proclaimed Russia to be a republic.

The Kerensky government was located in Petrograd in the old imperial palace from which it governed. For a few months, February through October, two opposing groups ran the government. One was the Provisional Government, which superseded the Tsar, i.e., the Kerensky Government, and that which was loyal to the Petrograd Soviet (Council) of Workers' Deputies, an early form of the communist government that emerged in October of 1917 with Vladimir Lenin at the helm.

Because of the continuing political unrest and the increasing power of the Bolsheviks, another revolution took place in November of 1917 (October, 1917 by the Julian calendar).

Vladimir Lenin led the Bolsheviks to victory by occupying the palace on or about October 25th of 1917 by the Julian calendar.

Historians tell us Kerensky fled the palace by automobile and eventually settled in the United States, where he lived until his death.

With the chronology of the Bolshevik Revolution behind us, let's briefly review some of the political, economic, and social issues encountered by the people of Russia at that time.

First, consider they had been at war with Germany for a few years (World War I). The Russians were tired of the war and were ready to support anyone who would promise them a way out of their circumstances.

They were working sixty to seventy hours a week and living in crowded housing conditions.[1]

Vladimir Lenin, leader of the Bolsheviks, promised the Russian people "Peace! Land! Bread!" He also promised the people hope and change if they allowed him to have the children for eight years, after which they would be Bolsheviks forever. He accomplished the goal through the school system. The education system became one of indoctrination. Our education system is following the same path by omitting our history which connects us to the Judeo-Christian ethic.

"Peace, Land, Bread" met the three basic desires of the Russian people. "Peace" meant ending Russian involvement in World War I. "Land" meant the abolition of private property and a redistribution of land to the peasants who worked the land (right out of the *Communist Manifesto*). "Bread" meant an end to widespread food shortages.[2] This is reminiscent of the promise of "Hope and Change" given by President Obama in his presidential campaign of 2008. He's using the mantra again in his campaign of 2012, as well.

Lenin died in 1924 and Joseph Stalin assumed the reins of the Russian Communist Party.

The Russian people received none of Lenin's promises, as have we, in the United States, received none of the Hope and Change the electorate had envisioned based on the promises of President Obama. The only change we've seen is one from a capitalist republican democracy to one of a socialist oligarchy at best, to a socialist autocracy at worst, in which the Constitution of the United States is no more than a convenient slogan. That, of course, was the hope and change Obama meant, not what the voters thought it would be.

1. Wikipedia: What did Lenin and the Bolsheviks promise the people of Russia? The parenthetical phrase is mine.
2. Ibid

Fast Forward to 1946

At this point, I'm going to give you an abridged version of a book, ...*and not a shot is fired* by Jan Kozak, who was a leader of the Czechoslovakian Communist Party from 1945 until his death. The book is no longer in print and the former publisher gave me permission to do an abridgement from a .pdf file found on line.

This book is the blueprint for a *legislative* takeover of a parliamentary government by perfectly subversive legal means. The similarity to our current circumstances in the U. S. are frightening.

...and not a shot is fired

by
Jan Kozak

(Member of the Secretariat of the Communist Party of Czechoslovakia)

Robert Welch University Press
Appleton, Wisconsin
08/12/10

The publisher gratefully acknowledges the generous contribution of The MacPherson Charitable Trust, which helped to make this RWU Press edition of *And Not a Shot Is Fired* a reality.

New 1999 edition with foreword by Thomas R. Eddlem and index not in the original.

Originally published in Czech under the title: *How Parliament Can Play a Revolutionary Part in the Transition to Socialism and the Role of the Popular Masses*

Published by Robert Welch University Press
P.O. Box 8050
Appleton, Wisconsin 54913
Printed in the United States of America
Library of Congress Catalog Card Number: 99-071272
ISBN: 1-892647-01-X

Introduction

ONE might ask today, years after the fall of the Berlin Wall: "Why would anyone want to read a report by a communist about the revolutionary takeover of Czechoslovakia — a country that no longer exists? The Czechs are capitalists now, remember?"

Such a question reveals a number of erroneous assumptions that this document convincingly refutes — not the least of which is the false assumption that the leaders of the former Communist states of

Eastern Europe were wedded to ideology. As Jan Kozak and 40 years of brutal Communist Party rule in Czechoslovakia so clearly demonstrate, communism was a tactic employed for the assumption of power, rather than a sincere belief. These same tactics, modified only slightly, are being used today. Americans who labor under the false premise that communism is either an ideology or a system of economics that died with the Cold War do so at their personal and national peril.

Most Americans are falsely conditioned to believe today that elective governments are permanently established and practically invincible to destruction, so long as elections are free from fraud and consumers can buy Big Mac hamburgers in the market. *And Not a Shot Is Fired* authoritatively disproves that myth. This document is a "how-to" manual for totalitarian takeover of an elected parliamentary system of government through mainly *legal and constitutional* means. Kozak did not pontificate fuzzy theories of how "revolutionary parliamentarianism" might be accomplished. He wrote from personal experience and intimate knowledge of how this seizure of power *actually was accomplished*. Kozak's manual is especially important for contemporary Americans because most of the same methods described in this book are at work in the United States today, although those methods are not being followed directly under communist ideological auspices. More on that, after a little background.

Origin of the Document

And Not A Shot Is Fired only accidentally made it into the public domain. Written between 1950 and 1955 (and revised somewhat after that) as an internal Czechoslovak Communist Party strategy paper, the two chapters which comprise this document were discussed briefly by Communist Czechoslovak delegates to the Inter-Parliamentary Union (IPU) in London in the fall of 1957. Kozak was a member of the Czechoslovak Communist Party Central Committee, briefly a member of the government secretariat, and later, official historian for the Czechoslovak Communist Party. A copy of these two chapters, officially entitled *How Parliament Can Play a Revolutionary Part in the Transition to Socialism and The Role of the Popular Masses*, were requested through IPU channels by British delegates to the conference. The word came back from the

11

Czechoslovaks that the just-published manuscript was mysteriously "out of print." It was not until January of 1961 that, according to the original British publishers, "by a mere coincidence, a copy of the report was secured." 1

Once received, Kozak's manifesto was quickly translated into English and published in February of that year by London's Independent Research Centre under a combination of the titles Kozak had given them: *How Parliament Can Play a Revolutionary Part in the Transition to Socialism and the Role of the Popular Masses*. The document became an instant international sensation, and by the beginning of 1962 Kozak's manual was being widely distributed in several languages throughout Europe and the United States. Radio Free Europe (RFE) published its own English translation under the original title, and a committee of Congress reproduced and distributed the RFE translation as well. It is the RFE translation (as published by Congress) which we have reproduced here.

But most Americans who came to know Jan Kozak and his step-by-step program for a totalitarian takeover of a free government read the book under the title *And Not A Shot Is Fired*, under which the Connecticut-based Long House publishers distributed the original British translation of Kozak's manual. The title of the popular American edition came straight out of the superb introduction by John Howland Snow. Snow explained that Kozak's document is a blueprint of how a "representative government can be made authoritarian, legally, piece by piece. The form remains, an empty shell.... *And not a shot is fired.*"2

Americans with only a little knowledge of post-war Europe are under the illusion that after the defeat of Hitler, Stalin installed his lackeys in Eastern European governments solely by force of the Soviet Army. This was not the case. Stalin had to pledge at least the appearance of free elections at Yalta, even if the concessions granted by Franklin D. Roosevelt guaranteed the eventual absorption of Eastern Europe into Stalin's orbit.

Eastern Europe actually enjoyed a short period of relative freedom after the war, during 1946 and 1947, when there were more or less free elections. Most of the Soviet-occupied countries elected non-communist majorities, despite severe harassment of noncommunist parties during the election campaigns. This document explains how, after the elections in Czechoslovakia, the Communist Party insinuated itself into a coalition with Social Democrats and gained control of the Agricultural and Interior ministries.

The value of this book is not that it explained "new" techniques or strategies for taking over free governments. There was nothing original in the strategies and tactics for taking over free governments outlined by Kozak, although many Americans in the 1960s — even among those who thought they were well informed — regarded Kozak's blueprint as new tactics and ideology. In fact, most of what Kozak describes had been theorized a generation earlier by Italian Communist Party chief Antonio Gramsci. But only Kozak has demonstrated how such a takeover actually was accomplished. *And Not A Shot Is Fired* has enduring value for several reasons, not the least of which is that the brief treatise is sufficiently straightforward — and comparatively free of communistic dialectical jargon — that it can be profitably read by the casual reader. That the document was written in a form readily comprehensible by the lay reader can only be chalked up to Communist overconfidence in the inevitable ascendancy of their empire. Kozak boasted that the Communist empire "comprises over 25 per cent of the whole world; 35 per cent of the world's population lives in it and about 30 per cent of the world's industrial output is produced by it." (Page 1) To be sure, Jan Kozak prolifically used communistic patois throughout the manual, drawing from a lexicon that has been alternatively termed "dialectics," "wordsmanship," and "Aesopean language." And the document can be read much more profitably with a thorough knowledge of the Communist Party's dialectic of that time frame. But Kozak's manuscript is one of those rare specimens of totalitarian literature where the main thrust of the document is understandable on its face even without that knowledge.

Ideology as a Tactic, Not a Belief
The one, overriding goal stressed by Kozak was the objective of seizing total power.
There is no concern for the lot of the poor, or the conditions of the laborer, or even the wealth of the industrialist evident in this manuscript; power is the one and only goal:

13

The overall character of the participation in this government was: not to lose sight, even for a moment, the carrying out of a complete socialist coup. (Page 12)

By using these methods, this principle was fulfilled in practice: not to lose sight for a single moment of the aim of a complete socialist overthrow. (Page 18)

[T]he following may and must be carried out successfully ... concentration of all power in the hands of the [communist-dominated] parliament." (Page 38)

In the course of the fight for the complete takeover of all power... (Page 39)

It's [the Communist Party's] aim was ... the definite settlement of the question of power by
consolidating people's democracy into a state of the dictatorship of the proletariat. (Page 46)

There are more passages in the book about how the leaders of the Czechoslovak Communist Party sought dictatorial power for themselves, but the murderous 40forty-year reign of this criminal syndicate (a criminal syndicate clothed with the pretended legitimacy of state power) makes further elucidation unnecessary. Kozak was no dreamy-eyed professor embracing a nebulous idea of a future socialist utopia; he and his confederates were reality-hardened schemers who would use any method available to gain as much power as possible. To power-hungry conspirators like Kozak, Communist ideology was mainly a useful cover for the organizational undertaking of a coup d'etat — a tactic, not a belief system. The Communists actually disdained other socialists, such as social democrats, even though they constantly strove to coalesce with and co-opt these democratic parties.

Co-opting Ideological Language
The Communists adapted the language of socialist ideology and the political policies of socialist regimes for their own internal use on several fronts. Many socialist terms were given double meanings — sometimes called "dialectics" — among Communist revolutionaries for furtherance of their coup. Thus, terms like "proletariat" and

"worker's class" can have their plain meaning or be code words for "Communist Party leaders." Or, "people's interest," "democratic will of the masses," and "decision of the proletariat" could have its ordinary meaning or designate "orders from Party leadership."

The use of dialectic meaning in words was and remains a necessary part of any plan to overthrow free governments. Outright announcement of the goals and motivations of revolutionaries would arouse too much alarm among the people and create too much resistance, resulting in the defeat of the conspirators. The use of such double-meaning terms serves as a means of transmitting, indirectly, an action program to fellow conspirators without alarming the general populace. If confronted with the true dialectical meaning of the terms, conspirators can simply claim that it is merely ideological belief, and that the accuser is simply a paranoid who is falsely reading sinister motivations into the revolutionary's words.

Dialectical speech was not unique to Kozak's Czechoslovak branch of the Communist Party, nor has it been limited to Communism. Mafiosi and other criminal gangs typically have their own language that serves both as verbal handshakes and to communicate without attracting the notice of the law. And, like the lingo of gangsters, Communist dialectics changes frequently in order to preserve its esoteric qualities. (Few would think that "wise guys" today would utilize antiquated terms such as "rubbed out," "greased," or "squeezed" anymore, because they have long been in the common parlance.)

In Communist history, dialectical "code-speech" goes all the way back to the beginning. As far back as 1848, when Karl Marx and Friedrich Engels completed *The Communist Manifesto,* it was widely condemned as being a conspiratorial document. Few literate men then took seriously Marx and Engels' preposterous claim that the government-power grab which comprised the ten-plank platform in *The Communist Manifesto* would lead to what the two later promised as the "withering away" of the state.3 To claim that the state withers away when you give it more power requires profound stupidity or brazen dishonesty. And, by all accounts, Marx and Engels were not stupid. *The Communist Manifesto*, like Kozak's manuscript, is simply a manual of how to take control of a government, the latter having laid out the scheme in both more openly brazen terms and greater mechanical detail.

Tactical "Ideology" for Would-Be Dictators: Socialism

To a Communist conspirator like Kozak, socialist ideology offered advantages beyond mere discreet communication with fellow revolutionaries. Revolutionaries frequently promote socialism because a socialist economy — even socialism under a parliamentary system of government— heavily concentrates power in the hands of the few people who run the state. Concentration of power in the hands of a few government leaders makes the state easier to seize by a determined conspiracy. To conspirators, socialism serves as a control-the-wealth program, not a share-the-wealth program. Thus, none should be surprised that Hitler and Mussolini took over freely-elected parliaments in their countries-—legally and constitutionally, as Kozak and his co=conspirators later accomplished only after posing as socialist ideologues of one form or another.

Some may contest the assertion that Hitler and Mussolini arose out of socialism because of popular notions that these dictators stem from the "right" wing of the ideological spectrum. Such illusions have no basis in fact. The very name "Nazi" was almost never used by the Nazis themselves; it was merely an acronym for Hitler's "National Socialist Party" that created such socialist institutions as the government automobile industry. (Volkswagen, which originated as a government program under the Hitler regime, means "people's car" in German.) And Mussolini's deep socialist roots date back to before World War I, with his editorship of the socialist newspaper, *Avanti!* From a power politics perspective Mussolini's fascism, after being imposed upon Italy, differed only superficially with outright socialism. Mussolini had completely adopted the notion that government should be fully involved in controlling property, even if he did allow nominal private ownership.

Il Duce's program that the state would be the "supreme regulator of the relations between all citizens of the state"[4] fits hand-in-glove with the political program instituted by Kozak and his co=conspirators after they had taken power for themselves. Economic fascism, which is simply heavy government regulation and control of what is only nominally private property, serves essentially the same purpose for conspirators as outright government ownership under socialism. And

16

fascism is the economic program increasingly being followed in the United States, and the formerly socialist nations of Eastern Europe, today. Economic fascism offers a number of advantages for the modern conspirator over the socialism used by Kozak but only because fascism is typically called some other nebulous name such as "Third Way" or "public-private partnership," or (even worse) falsely represented as "privatization," or "free trade," or "free enterprise." The fascist economic model does not carry all the public relations baggage of Stalinist socialism, and, over the short term at least, it can be more economically efficient than outright socialism.* Thus, it should be no surprise that the same conspirators who ran the governments of former Soviet "Republics" of Eastern Europe have readily exchanged their Communist Party posts for "elective" posts, or that the brand of state control they are now pushing is called "privatization" and "economic reform."

Pressure from Above, Pressure from Below

A socialist or fascist economic policy is necessary for dictatorial revolution in an elective government and not simply because socialism or fascism concentrates the physical power of the state in the few who run the executive branch of government. While these policies certainly enable the state to acquire power (and to shift power away from the legislature) their chief role as necessary ingredients for revolution is that they give the state hegemonic control (leadership) over the various non=governmental cultural institutions—institutions which may have enough strength to resist and overthrow a political coup d'etat. Kozak uses an excellent example in this text of the hegemonic leadership manufactured by the Communists over agriculture in Czechoslovakia. Farmers and ranchers have traditionally been very conservative, independent, and resistant to tyranny. In a heavily agricultural state such as war-devastated Czechoslovakia, farmers and ranchers would have been a strong counter-revolutionary force. Indeed, Stalin had found farmers to be the chief anti-totalitarian force in pre-war Ukraine.

But in Czechoslovakia, Communist cadres "from below" infiltrated and co-opted the conservative leadership of the agricultural interests, giving the misleading impression that farmers were divided on the revolution, or perhaps even supportive of it. Meanwhile, "parliamentary socialism"—the "pressure from above"—used the

17

power of the state, under the pretext of yielding to pressure from "farmers" (represented by these Communist infiltrators) to break up the economic base and strength of the independent farmers.

As the preceding example illustrates, Kozak outlined the main thesis of a giant pincer's strategy for transforming a parliamentary system of government into a totalitarian dictatorship—the strategy of combining "pressure from above" with "pressure from below" to effect revolutionary change. In essence, under this plan, the Communist minority in parliament (in coalition with socialist parties) serves the revolution by initiating policies and legislation which strengthen the hand of grassroots revolutionaries and punish threats to the coup (i.e., the Right). Meanwhile, grassroots revolutionaries whip up the appearance of popular support for the legislative program to advance the revolution through strikes, rallies, petitions, threats, and sometimes — sabotage. The "pressure from below" by the small number of revolutionaries and their larger number of dupes is then used to "justify" the centralization of power in the hands of the executive branch of the state. Wishy-washy politicians are intimidated, and the "pressure from above" intensifies. Each legislative victory results in new demands (the "pressure from below") for even stronger legislation, which is relentlessly pursued by communists and their dupes in parliament who claim, of course, that they are acting in the name of the popular will. The cycle continues until opposition is completely powerless, intimidated, or liquidated and the revolution is a *fait accompli.*

 The theory for using "pressure from above" and "pressure from below" in order to acquire power, explained in this manual by Kozak, first emerged in the writings of an obscure Italian Communist thinker named Antonio Gramsci. Gramsci had plenty of time for contemplating the reasons why his Communist Party had lost Italy to Benito Mussolini, since he spent the last years of his life in Mussolini's jails. Gramsci concluded that in order to capture the power in a state, one must first capture the culture. By culture, Gramsci meant the powerful non-governmental institutions of great influence throughout the nation, specifically: churches, unions, mass media, political parties, universities and educational centers, business organizations, foundations, etc. Gramsci explained that, in hindsight, it was unreasonable to expect the Communists to have seized power in pre-World War II Italy in the same way that the October Revolution had succeeded in Russia.

"In [totalitarian, Tsarist] Russia the state was everything," Gramsci explained in his *Prison Notebooks*. "[C]ivil society was primordial and gelatinous; in the West, there was a proper relation between state and civil society, and when the state trembled a sturdy structure of civil society was at once revealed."[5]

In the West, Gramsci explained, family loyalties, faith in God, and lawful limits on governmental power were thoroughly represented in the cultural institutions. Gramsci wrote that "there can and must be a 'political hegemony' even before assuming government power, and in order to exercise political leadership or hegemony one must not count solely on the power and material force that is given by government."[6] Gramsci argued that without a successful "war of position" for "cultural hegemony" (cultural leadership) within these institutions, a revolutionary power grab — even by a well organized conspiracy — is impossible. Ultimately, the Italian Communists were outmaneuvered in the cultural war by Mussolini's blackshirts. *Belief in God, family, and limited government in the developed nations of the West constitutes a cultural system of "fortresses and earthworks" against revolution, according to Gramsci. A coup d'etat, without having first subverted these "fortresses and earthworks" through the acquisition of political/cultural hegemony, would only be temporary and result in a quick and successful counter revolution.* The revolutionaries of today are well aware that their struggle for control of the culture cannot be won overnight. Gramsci follower and Frankfort school of socialism apostle Rudi Dutschke explained the Gramscian struggle as a "long march through the institutions"[7] to win Gramsci's "war of position" over any cultural institutions which would stand in the way of a coup d'etat by a conspiratorial faction.

To revolutionaries like Kozak and Gramsci, all cultural and governmental institutions constitute battlefields. Kozak explained that the Czech Communist Party created "mass organizations" to form that pressure from below, and used the power of the state to take over, eliminate, or isolate the old conservative institutions: "[T]he 'pressure from above' was applied in an ever-increasing measure for the direct suppression and destruction of the counter-

19

revolutionary machinations of the bourgeoisie [the middle class]. Let us recall the signal role played in the development and extension of that pressure by the Ministry of the Interior, for instance, which was led by the Communists and the units of the State Security directed by them." (Page 13) As the state passed draconian gun control laws throughout Eastern European countries in the aftermath of World War II, the Communist Party armed itself and — together with its control of the police organs of government — obtained a monopoly on force in these nations. "The necessity of arming the most mature part of the workers' class for repulsing the counter-revolutionary machinations of the bourgeoisie ... has been proved, incidentally, again by the later formation of the workers' militias in peoples' democratic Hungary and Poland," Kozak emphasized. (Page 25) That victorious revolutionaries would need a monopoly on force to consolidate control of a country is an obvious necessity, and it highlights our Second Amendment-protected right to keep and bear arms as an obvious "earthwork" against revolution. But in Czechoslovakia, it should be emphasized, the monopoly on force mainly served a more subtle purpose than a violent overthrow; it created a helpless feeling among the increasingly isolated non-communist opposition. The clash of arms was never necessary.

Many elements of the "pressure from above" and "pressure from below" stratagem explained by Kozak are being used against Americans on a variety of fronts toward the consolidation of power in the hands of the state. Kozak explained that the revolution also "breaks through the onerous circle of intimidation and spiritual terror of the old institutions, the Church, etc." (Page 19) Modern activists and would-be revolutionaries attempt to isolate and outmaneuver those churches that cling to traditional teachings by (for example) using Kozak's tactics to effect change on the issue of birth control and abortion. Both the U.S. government and the United Nations (as well as tax-exempt foundations) fund private organizations such as Planned Parenthood that perform abortions and distribute birth control devices. At the same time, these organizations lobby governments and create the appearance of popular support for government-subsidized abortion on demand and (eventually) coercive population-control programs. The United Nations uses a Non-Governmental Organization (NGO) caucus of left-wing organizations to create grassroots (pressure from below) to justify its authoritarian agenda, which (on the population-control front) includes support for China's population-control program of forced abortion. The NGOs, of course, by no means represent the grassroots. But that does not prevent the movers and shakers at the top, including the foundation heads and governmental officials who lavishly fund them, from representing them as such. There are dozens of other modern examples of how the "pressure from above" has created and funded the "pressure from below," from the environmentalist movement to the international gun control movement—the details of which could fill many pages.

The U.S. Constitution — a formidable "earthwork"

The U.S. Constitution — by way of contrast with parliamentary socialism/fascism — offers a formidable series of barriers to would-be dictators, with its separation of powers, system of checks and balances, reserved rights, delegated powers, and free enterprise based economy. James Madison explained in The Federalist, #47, that the division of powers in the U.S. Constitution was devised with the following guiding principle of politics constantly in mind: "The accumulation of all powers, legislative, executive, and judiciary, in the same hands, whether of one, a few, or many, and whether hereditary, self-appointed, or elective, may justly be pronounced the very definition of tyranny." Gramsci strongly felt that "the whole liberal [i.e., classical, laissez-faire liberalism] ideology, with its strengths and weaknesses, can be summed up in the principle of the division of powers, and the source of liberalism's weakness becomes apparent: it is the bureaucracy, i.e. the crystallization of the leading personnel, which exercises coercive power..."[8] In other words, Gramsci was saying that revolutionaries can make use of ambitious individual politicians — who need not necessarily be revolutionaries at first — to usurp power and break down the division of powers which limits government in constitutional systems. Madison concurred in "The Federalist, #10," that the main problem in free governments was the tendency to faction and ambition among the ruling personalities. "The friend of popular governments never finds himself so much alarmed for their character and fate as when he contemplates their propensity to this dangerous vice," the Father of the Constitution explained. But the Founders constructed the U.S. Constitution to ameliorate this very problem. As Alexander Hamilton explained in The Federalist, #9:

21

"The regular distribution of power into distinct departments; the introduction of legislative balances and checks; the institution of courts composed of judges holding their offices during good behavior; the representation of the people in the legislature by deputies of their own election: these are wholly new discoveries, or have made their principal progress towards perfection in modern times. They are means, and powerful means, by which the excellencies of republican government may be retained and its imperfections lessened or avoided."

What Can Be Done?

To a large extent, many of our cultural and governmental institutions have already been captured by forces in favor of the centralization of government power and, opposed to limited government and the traditional morality of the churches. Few Americans are even aware that an invasion of our institutions has been ongoing or that the invaders have won several engagements. Author and political commentator John T. Flynn has already been proven partly right in his 1941 warning that "We will not recognize [American totalitarianism] as it rises. It will wear no black shirts here. It will probably have no marching songs. It will rise out of a congealing of a group of elements that exist here and that are the essential components of Fascism.... It will be at first decorous, humane, glowing with homely American sentiment."9 Several of the constitutional "fortresses and earthworks" which the Founding Fathers threw up to block revolution in our constitutional system have given way to decay in recent decades. The marginalization of gun ownership through federal legislation, the progressive lack of respect for the federal system of states rights by both political parties, and the assault on free speech rights protected by the First Amendment through so-called "campaign finance reform" are but a few of many examples. Part of the "long march through the institutions" has already been completed.

But it is not yet too late. There are still cultural and structural layers of "fortresses and earthworks" which continue to protect Americans against the kind of quasi-legal revolution this book outlines. There are still some checks and balances and division of powers left in our system, and there is still vigorous organizational opposition to consolidation of governmental powers. But these defenses are under siege. The only way to guarantee continued free government is for

Americans to get active in restoring those political and cultural "fortresses and earthworks" which support the principles James Madison and the rest of the founders put into the U.S. Constitution. We can guard this principle of the division of powers by insisting—both directly and especially through those cultural institutions where we can have any influence—that our elected officials revive the separation of powers and consistently vote for a reduction in the size and scope of government.

Thomas R. Eddlem
Appleton, WI
January, 1999

Endnotes to the Introduction

[1] Lord Morrison of Lambeth, Introduction to How Parliament Can Play a Revolutionary Part in the Transition to Socialism and the Role of the Popular Masses (London: Independent Information Centre, 1961), 9th edition, pp. 3-4.

[2] John Howland Snow, Introduction to And Not a Shot Is Fired (New Caanan, CT: The Long House, Inc., 1972), pp. 8-9.

[3] See, for example, Engels in 1878: Frederick Engels, Herr Eugen Duhring's Revolution in Science (New York: International Publishers, 1939), p. 307. Also, Marx was on record having said much the same thing in his 1875 "Critique of the Gotha Program": Karl Marx: Selected Writings in Sociology & Social Philosophy, (New York: McGraw-Hill, 1964), p. 256.

[4] Benito Mussolini, My Autobiography (New York: Charles Scribner's Sons, 1928) p. 280.

[5] Roger Simon, Gramsci's Political Thought (London: Lawrence and Wishart, 1982), p. 28.

[6] Antonio Gramsci, Prison Notebooks, Volume I (New York: Columbia University Press, 1992), p.137.

[7] Richard Grenier, Capturing the Culture (Washington, DC: Ethics and Public Policy Center, 1991), p. xlv.

[8] Antonio Gramsci, The Modern Prince and Other Writings (New York: International Publishers, 1959), p.186.

[9] John T. Flynn, "Coming: A Totalitarian America" (originally appearing in the February 1941 American Mercury), in Forgotton Lessons (Irvington-on-Hudson, NY: Foundation for Economic Education, 1996), pp. 142-143.

Main Text

...and not a shot is fired

How Parliament Can Play a Revolutionary Part in the Transition to Socialism and The Role of the Popular Masses

by Jan Kozak
Translated from the original Czech

Publisher's note: This document was originally published in the Czech language, and the following is an exact replication of the translation from the U.S. government's Radio Free Europe and published by the House Committee on Un-American Activities of the 87th Congress. For the purposes of clarity and better readability, we have added subheadings, changed italics, and adjusted arbitrary spaces between paragraphs.

THE classics of Marxism-Leninism never ceased to point out the inexorable revolutionary transformation of the capitalist society into a socialist one does not preclude, but even presupposes the possibility of various forms and roads of the proletarian revolution. V. I. Lenin, in particular, illuminated this serious question thoroughly and systematically. In his lifetime the proletarian revolution became an immediate question of the day. In his theoretical works and concretely in his practical activity he started from the principle that the forms of transition to socialism are dependent on the concrete balance of international and internal class forces, on the degree of organization of the proletariat and the bourgeoisie, on the ability to gain allies, the level of the economic structure and on the political traditions and forms of the organizations.

From the moment the Great Socialist October Revolution broke the chains of imperialism and gave power to the relatively weak proletariat of the nations of backward Russia, profound objective and subjective changes began to take place in the world. The present fruit of the Socialist October Revolution is the new historical era, **the characteristic feature of which lies in the origin and consolidation of the socialist global constellation**. This constellation now embraces 17 countries, with the USSR and China at its head; it comprises over 25 per cent of the whole world; 35 per cent of the world's population lives in it and about 30 per cent of the world's industrial output is produced by it.

24

The second characteristic feature of this new historical era is the collapse of the colonial system as a world factor. Important Asian and African countries such as India, Indonesia, Burma, Egypt and others have cast off the shackles of imperialism.

Both these main characteristics of the new historical era — the origin of the socialist constellation and the collapse of the colonial system — have profoundly changed the objective structure of the world. These profound changes in the objective structure of the world are necessarily accompanied also by profound subjective changes — changes in the thinking, views, political and practical orientation of the broad popular masses. ...These trends, which are the result and the product of the new subjective processes in society, are, however, dispersed, isolated and constantly weakened by the propaganda of the ruling bourgeoisie and by the ideology and practice of reformism. In a number of capitalist and dependent countries there still slumbers the enormous, but still dispersed force of the broad popular masses. The workers' class is faced with the task of firmly taking a stand at the head of the struggle for the national and democratic interests of its respective nations, of uniting in its fight for socialism and of creating, under its leadership, a united and mighty anti-imperialist popular movement.

The new historical era and its tasks have created most favorable conditions for the workers' class in this way for gaining new allies. The old tenets about the allies of the workers' class which corresponded to old historical conditions are undergoing a change and are widening. Along with the changed conditions for the struggle for national democratic and peace interests, the conditions for the struggle of the workers' class for socialism are also changing. In the fight against imperialism, which endeavors to overcome its conflicts by completely ignoring the interests of the nations and which strives to liquidate their independence as states, the national role of the workers' class is growing and it is placed in the forefront of all patriotic and democratic forces.

Patriotism: A Difficulty for the Proletarian Revolution

"Patriotism," V. I. Lenin proclaimed, "is one of the deepest feelings firmly rooted in the hearts of people for hundreds and thousands of years from the moment their separate fatherlands began to exist. It has been one of the greatest, one can say exceptional, difficulties of our proletarian revolution that it had to pass through a period of sharpest conflict with patriotism during the time of the Brest-Litovsk peace." (V. I. Lenin, "Spisy" Vol. 28, Czech edition, 1955, p. 187.)

Parliament as "an instrument ... of the socialist revolution"

The new conditions which are the consequence of the profound objective and subjective changes in the world create new opportunities and prospects for the socialist revolution.

Our experience provides notable and practical proof that it is possible to transform parliament from an instrument of the bourgeoisie into an instrument of the revolutionary democratic will of the people and into an instrument for the development of the socialist revolution.

When the German imperialist occupiers, aided by the treacherous bourgeoisie at home and with the consent of the Western imperialist powers, destroyed the national liberty and the independence of the Czechoslovak republic in 1938 and 1939, the Communist Party of Czechoslovakia (hereinafter CPCS) placed itself at the head of the struggle for national liberation by the Czech and Slovak people.

Hitler's Germany was crushed by the armies of the Soviet Union and that our country was directly liberated by the Soviet army, that national and democratic revolution conquered. As a consequence the occupation power of the German imperialists and of their domestic helpmates — the treacherous financial, industrial and agrarian upper bourgeoisie — was swept away, national unity and independence as a state was revived and a deep-reaching democratization of the country was carried out. Furthermore, the sovereignty and independence of Czechoslovakia was renewed in the form of a new, people's democratic order.

The Communist Party Consolidates Its Influence

In this struggle the workers' class, led by the CPCS, became the recognized driving force of the nation; its action-unity was consolidated and the influence of reformism which had splintered it in the years of the pre-Munich republic was weakened. The victory of the national and democratic revolution meant for the workers' class, which had relied in this struggle on all patriotic and democratic forces — the peasants, tradesmen, the intelligentsia and part of the Czech and Slovak bourgeoisie — its access to power.

The workers' class was the main force in the new revolutionary democratic government (the so-called Kosice Government) and in the national committees — the new organs of the state's power created from below by the revolutionary masses.

Of the political points in this program, these were the most important: the breaking up of the basic members of the old oppressive bourgeois state apparatus and assumption of power by the national committees, the formation of a new people's security system and army, the prohibition of the revival of the political parties which had represented the treacherous upper bourgeoisie, a systematic purge of the entire political, economic and cultural life of the country, the settlement of the relations between the Czech and Slovak nations on the principle of equality, the expulsion of the German minority, etc.

Changing the Social Structure
Of the economic measures, the following were the most important: the transfer of all enemy property, of that of the treacherous upper bourgeoisie and of other traitors, to the national administration of the new people's authority; the transfer of the land belonging to these enemies and traitors to the ownership of landless persons, tenants and working smallholders.

All these measures, aiming at far-reaching changes in the social structure of the country, emanated directly from the conditions and tasks of the anti-fascist, national and democratic fight for liberation and arose from the old democratic traditions and longing of our people and they, furthermore, deepened and safeguarded that democracy.

As early as the end of the summer of 1945, after agreement had been reached between the political parties forming the National Front, the Provisional National Assembly was elected (on the principle of parity representation) and, in May 1946, the Constituent National Assembly in general, secret, direct and fair elections. The composition of

27

Parliament was strongly influenced by the results of the revolution, by the practical schooling of the working masses in the course of the victorious revolution.

The workers' class, whose struggle had made it possible that this institution could be re-established, strove for Parliament, as one of the most prominent political traditions and forms of the past, to change its character (lit.: content; Tr.), to change it from an instrument of the workers' class into one of the levers actuating the further development and consolidation of the revolution, into a direct instrument for the socialist building of the country. The bourgeoisie, on the other hand, strove for Parliament to be revised with its old content — bourgeois parliamentarianism — and tried to use it for the stopping of the revolution, for the demolition of its achievements, for the consolidation and widening of its former political and economic power positions, for the preparation of the restoration of its former rule and dictatorship.

Parliament Provides "Pressure From Above"
This struggle took place during the period from 1946-1948. In the course of these years the workers' class, led by the Communists, made effective use of all its old forms of fighting, employed by the revolutionary workers' parties in Parliament, adjusted, however to the new conditions, and found new ones. Helped by Parliament, which was used by the workers' class for deepening the revolution and for the gradual, peaceful and bloodless change of the national and democratic revolution into a socialist one as "pressure from above," and by its effect on the growth of the "pressure from below," the bourgeoisie was pushed step by step from its share in the power. This gradual and bloodless driving of the bourgeoisie from power and the quite legitimate constitutional expansion of the power of the workers' class and of the working people was completed in February 1948 by the parliamentary settlement of the government crisis engineered by the bourgeoisie.

Parliament underwent a change. *The form remained but the content was different.* Our working people, led by the Communists, provided practical proof during the years 1945-1948 that it was possible to transform parliament from an organ of the bourgeoisie into an instrument developing democratic measures of consequence, leading

28

to the gradual change of the social structure and into a direct instrument for the victory of the socialist revolution.

From Capitalism to Socialism — By Means of Parliament

This fact, coupled with similar experiences gained by the other Communist and workers' parties, led to the possibility being envisaged of the transition of some countries from capitalism to socialism by revolutionary use of parliament. This was most clearly illuminated and generalized at the 20th Congress of the CPSU shows, *relying on the revolutionary activity of the masses. Such a government can be set up without armed battle, by peaceful means.*

The purpose to which this new power, the nucleus of which would be formed by the workers' class, should be put thereafter would be the use of parliament for the consolidation and deepening of the real democratic rights and to a more or less speedy unfolding of the socialist revolution (Generally our tasks during the years 1945-1948). The use of parliament *itself* for the transfer of all power into the hands of the workers' class, and would always correspond with the specific class and historical conditions.

Despite these differences there are in existence fundamental, conditions for the possibility of a revolutionary use of parliament on the road to socialism, the substance of which is revolutionary and which are to be clearly distinguished from the reformist conception of the aim and use of Parliament.

The most important of these lies in the necessity of combining the revolutionary activity of parliament with a systematic development and the organization of revolutionary actions on the part of broad popular masses.

The Combination of "Pressure From Above" and that "From Below" — One of the Elementary Conditions for the Revolutionary Use of Parliament.

A preliminary condition for carrying out fundamental social changes and for making it possible that parliament be made use of for the purpose of transforming a capitalist society into a socialist one, is: *(a) to fight for a firm parliamentary majority which would ensure and develop a strong pressure from "above," and (b) to see to it that this firm parliamentary majority should rely on the revolutionary activity of the broad working masses exerting pressure "from below."*

Pressure From Above
(a) Regarding Questions of Using Pressure from "Above"

In 1905, V. I. Lenin proclaimed:

1. "To restrict, as a principle, revolutionary actions to pressure from below and to forgo pressure from above, is anarchism.

2. "Whoever cannot grasp the new tasks in the era of revolution, the tasks of actions, from above, whoever cannot state the conditions for and the program of such actions, that person has no idea of the tasks of the proletariat in any democratic revolution.

3. *"The principle that it is not admissible for social democracy (i.e., the revolutionary-party of the proletariat) to take part, jointly with the bourgeoisie, in a provisional revolutionary government, that every such participation should rate as betrayal of the workers' class, is a principle of anarchism."* (V. I. Lenin, "Spisy," Vol. 8, Czech edition1954. p. 477.)

The Bolsheviks were to have participated in the envisaged provisional revolutionary government in the bourgeois democratic revolution in Russia in 1905, with this aim: to lead a heedless fight against all counter-revolutionary efforts and to protect the independent interests of the workers' class. *The overall character of the participation in this government was: not to lose from sight, even for a moment, the carrying out of a complete socialist coup.*

Suppressing the Counter-revolution

Pressure from "above" is, therefore, the pressure of a revolutionary government, parliament and the other organs of power in the state apparatus or its parts and it has, in substance, a dual effect — the direct suppression by power of the counter-revolution and its machinations and, at the same time, the exertion of pressure on the citizens, inciting and organizing them for the struggle for a further development of the revolution.

Our workers' class and the CPCS gained valuable experience from the course of the struggle from "above" and the various forms of application in the new conditions. What were the principal forms of pressure "from above" applied in the period of the transformation of our national and democratic revolution into a socialist one?

Step One: Isolating the Bourgeoisie

The first direction given to the pressure "from above," which our workers' class applied from its position of power in the organs and newly forming links of the apparatus of the people's democratic state, was a systematic fight against enemies, traitors and collaborators. *Gradually, as the national and democratic revolution changed into a socialist one, the pressure "from above" was applied in an ever-increasing measure for the direct suppression and destruction of the counter-revolutionary machinations of the bourgeoisie.* Let us recall the signal role played in the development and extension of that pressure by the Ministry of the Interior, for instance, which was led by the Communists and the units of State Security directed by them.

But also other organs of the state and of the state apparatus controlled by the Communists also served for the direct suppression of bourgeois sabotage and obstructionism. So, for instance, the *Ministry of Agriculture* quickly completed, by means of so-called "roving commissions" (lit.: flying commissions; Tr.) the confiscation of the land of enemies and traitors, which had been sabotaged in the autumn of 1946 by the bourgeoisie.

The organs holding powers and the components of the state controlled by Communists, became unusually effective levers for the defense of the revolutionary achievements of the people and for the further advancement of the revolution. They made it possible to suppress directly bourgeois counter-revolutionary elements (to render harmless their sabotage and subversion). They formed a mighty support and force furthering the revolution.

Step Two: Popularizing Revolutionary Demands

The second prong of the pressure "from above" successfully employed by our workers' class was the use made of the organs holding powers (the government, parliament, national committees) for bringing about a wide popularization of revolutionary demands and slogans. So, for instance, the government approved the "Program of Building"elaborated by the Communists, which, in its substance, was a program for the further transformation of the democratic revolution into a socialist one. Its passage was of immense

31

importance since the program of the next economic-political measures for advancing the revolution, elaborated by the Communists, became the program of the entire government.

This direction given to the pressure "from above," therefore, served particularly the wide popularization of the demands and slogans of the policy of the Communists designed for a speedy progress of the revolution. It served as a means for the revolutionary education and organization of the popular masses.

Step Three: Nationalizing the Economy

A particularly important and exceptionally effective way of the struggle "from above" lay in the utilization of economic political power positions, especially the nationalization of the banks, of banking, of key and big industries.

The economic power positions of the workers' class, represented by the nationalized sector of the country's economy, were a mighty lever for the development of pressure "from above." It made possible the suppression and, to a considerable extent, the paralyzing of bourgeois counter-revolutionary intrigues aimed at economic decline and chaos. On the other hand, these positions also made possible the exerting of "pressure" on the citizens and broad masses of the working people. The fast expansion of nationalized production and the resulting rise in the standard of living of working people presented examples in point showing the advantages of a nationalized and, in its substance, working-class-controlled and directed production; gave rise to revolutionary self-confidence and determination on the part of the working people and thus contributed to a still further isolation of the bourgeoisie.

This method of pressure "from above" was, therefore, a mighty pillar and force of the progressing (lit.: deepening; Tr.) revolution.

Step Four: Using Power to Silence Opposition

The fourth direction given to the pressure "from above" existed in the utilization of the organs holding power for the direct uncovering of the anti-people policy of the bourgeoisie, for the isolation of the reactionary bourgeois leadership of the other parties of the National Front.

The Communists made use of the national committees, Parliament, the government organs for sharp criticism leveled against the other parties and their representatives on the grounds of inconsistency and obstructionism regarding the fulfillment of the tasks accepted in the program (in Parliament, for instance, the criticism and uncovering of the anti-people activity of the Ministry of Justice which was controlled by the National Socialist Party, the uncovering of the obstructionist inactivity of the Ministry of Food, controlled by the rightist Social Democrat Majer, etc.). At the same time, these organs holding power were used for tabling further demands and proposals in favor of the working people and, in this way, the bourgeoisie and its minions were forced either to their acceptance or to an open showing of their anti-people's face. (How important for the isolation of the bourgeois leadership of the other parties of the National Front was the proposal of the Millionaires' Levy alone, tabled in the government by the Communists in 1947 and at first rejected by its majority!)

All the basic forms and actions involving pressure "from above" employed by our workers' class in the years 1945-1948 conformed, in the new circumstances, with the tasks allotted to the pressure "from above" as predicted by Lenin — a fight without quarter against all counter-revolutionary attempts and the defense of the independent interests of the working class. By using these methods this principle was fulfilled in practice: *not to lose sight for a single moment of the aim of a complete socialist overthrow.*
The struggle "from above" carried out by our workers' class in the years 1945-1948 meant making use of the positions held by the workers' class in the organs vested with powers, for weakening and isolating the bourgeoisie, for conquering its positions by the workers' class and for the consolidation of the revolutionary democratic people's power in the dictatorship of the proletariat.

These forms and actions of the struggle "from above" greatly enriched the tactical armament and experience of the international workers' movement.

Our practice and successes in the struggle "from above" made a trenchant contribution to the generalization of the experience gained

33

and toward outlining the possibilities of a revolutionary use of parliament during the transition to socialism.

Pressure From Below
(b) Questions of Utilizing Pressure "From Below"
To bring about a parliament which would cease to be a "soft-soap factory" and would become a revolutionary assembly of working people requires, however, a force constituting, maintaining, and actively assisting its revolutionary activity. This force, necessary for breaking the resistance of the reactionary bourgeoisie, exists in the pressure by the popular masses "from below." Whereas pressure "from above" is the pressure exerted by the organs of the state and of the state apparatus for the direct suppression, by power, of the counter-revolution which helps, at the same time, to rally and organize the popular masses for the fight for further progress of the revolution, pressure "from below" is the pressure exerted by the popular masses on the government, on parliament and on other organs holding power. This pressure takes effect mainly in three directions:

(a) it systematically supports the revolutionaries in the organs of power, enhances their strength and *makes up for numerical weakness;*
(b) it has a direct effect on limiting the influence and positions of waverers and enemies standing in the path of the further progress of the revolution;
(c) it awakens the forces of the people dormant for many years, their energy and self-confidence; *it breaks through the onerous circle of intimidation and spiritual terror of the old institutions, the Church, etc.*

The pressure "from below," the revolutionary emergence of the popular masses, is, therefore, essential for the success of every revolution.

When Lenin clarified the possibility of and conditions for the participation of the revolutionary workers' party in the provisional revolutionary government in 1905, at the height of the bourgeois democratic revolution in Russia, he sharply stressed: "We are obliged to influence the provisional revolutionary government from below in any event." (V. I Lenin, "Selected Writings," I, page 456.)

34

In 1936*, when the Seventh Congress of the Communist International elaborated the line of a united and popular front and the government possibilities of a united or popular front, the necessity of pressure brought to bear on such a government by the revolutionary masses was stressed:

"Since this movement of a united front is a militant movement against fascism and the reactionaries, it will be a constant movable force driving the government of the united front into the fight against the reactionary bourgeoisie . . . And the better this mass movement is organized from below, the broader the network of supra-party class organs of the united front in the factories, among the unemployed in the labor districts, among the little men in towns and villages, the more guarantees will exist against a possible rejection of the policy of the government of the united front." (G. Dimitrov, "Digest from Speeches and Articles," 1950, page 103.)

Communist Party Prescription: "Pressure From Below"
The principle and the necessity of using pressure from below by the popular masses, forming one of the fundamental possibilities of making revolutionary use of parliament, as mentioned at the 20th Congress of the CPSU, ties in fully with the old practice of the revolutionary workers' classes in parliament also in the new conditions. Therefore, the revolutionary workers' movement must bring pressure to bear from below on parliament and the government whenever it wishes to protect, consolidate and extend the achievements of the revolution.

Our workers' class and the CPCS gained valuable experience also from the waging of the fight "from below," and the various forms of its application. Of particular importance is the experience with the great variety of forms of directing the pressure "from below," guaranteeing for the CPCS the leadership of the workers' class and of the broad popular masses.

The very conception of the existing broad National Front contributed to attaining this end. It consisted not only of the political parties but also broad united national mass organizations, the establishment of which the CPCS achieved with the help of the revolutionary activity of the masses. These organizations reinforced the positions of the workers' class and the positions of left progressive democratic forces in the other parties of the National Front. The united mass organizations, which were led and influenced to a large extent by the Communists, represented, in this way, virtually the direct reserves of the Party. Through them the strong influence of the policy of the Communists also penetrated into the other political parties and thus the unity of the National Front was strengthened from below over the heads of the leaders.

Use of National Mass Organizations

Of quite exceptional importance was the origin of the United Revolutionary Trade Union Movement (ROH). ROH, as a class and socialist organization, consolidated the unity of the workers' class; it enhanced its revolutionary strength and weight and, under the leadership of the Communist Party, it used this strength most effectively for the fortification of the people's democratic power and for the advancement of the socialist revolution. A great help for the guidance and organization of the revolutionary fight of the peasants were the so-called "Peasants' Commissions," whose members could be only farmhands, tenant farmers and small and medium farmers from the ranks of applicants for land. This network of broad national mass organizations was used by the Communists for the popularization of their policy and slogans, and for engendering and organizing the initiative of the masses and for using the various forms and actions of the pressure "from below" for the purpose of implementing that policy.

Use of Protests, Demonstrations, and Strikes

The second experience gained in the struggle "from below" is the many-sided use of the proper forms of pressure exerted by the popular masses. These forms corresponded to the complicated class situation in the conditions prevailing under the people's democratic order, when the workers' class assumed power but the bourgeoisie still kept part of the power. On the one side, all the old proven forms of the struggle of the popular masses were employed, the forms which were in keeping with the revolutionary initiative and determination of the workers and matched the degree of resistance shown by the bourgeoisie: *calling of protest meetings, passing of resolutions, sending of delegations, organizing mass demonstrations and also, eventually using strikes, including general strikes* (when finally the open political clash with the bourgeoisie was brought about in February 1948).

 The strength and striking power of the individual actions of the pressure "from below" increased as need arose, and were safeguarded by exceptional organizational forms. An especially prominent role was played in this by the "Congresses of Factory Councils" and the "Congresses of Peasants' Commissions" (when the political crisis was resolved in Slovakia in the autumn of 1947; in the struggle for nationalization of private capitalist enterprises with over 50 employees and the entire domestic and foreign wholesale business; when the demand was pressed home for land reform above 50 hectares; and when the political crisis was settled in February 1948).

 On the other side, the Communists, aided by the network of national mass organizations (and by the pressure "from above" exerted by the organs holding powers, especially the national committees and the government), developed new forms of pressure "from below," meeting the situation when the workers' class was proceeding with the assumption of power. These forms must be particularly noted. They are the organization of a broad building movement on the basis of voluntary brigades (coal, harvest, machine, etc.), and the advancement of competition in production within the factory and on a statewide scale. These "constructive" forms of pressure "from below" fortified the overall position of the people's democratic state, paralyzed the efforts of the bourgeoisie to bring about an economic and political upheaval and, through their results (fast economic consolidation of the country and a rising standard of living of the working people), permanently entrenched and reinforced the power positions of the workers' class in the country.

 This third most valuable experience gained by our workers' class is pressure "from below," much emphasized by Lenin, that is to say *arming the proletariat*. (V. I. Lenin stressed, in his work "Two Tactics," two principal conditions for the pressure from below: the proletariat must be armed because the threat of a civil war exists, and the proletariat must be led by a revolutionary workers' Party.)

 The workers' class armed itself in the course of the national and democratic revolution. One part of it became the nucleus of a new

37

armed state apparatus, especially the security apparatus under the control of the Ministry of the Interior which was in the hands of the Communists.

The second part, the so-called Factory Guards, permanently secured the safety of the works. In February 1948, when the preparations for a counter-revolutionary conspiracy by the bourgeoisie were uncovered, strong, armed people's militias were formed.. (The necessity of arming the most mature part of the workers' class for repulsing the counterrevolutionary machinations of the bourgeoisie and for ensuring the undisturbed building of socialism has been proved, incidentally, again by the later formation of the workers' militias in people's democratic Hungary and Poland.)

The armed parts of the workers' class thus represented a very real and concrete form of the pressure "from below" directed against the counter-revolution and a very concrete and effective support for the workers' forces in the organs of the state.

The pressure of the popular masses "from below" (in the totality of all its forms and concrete actions) made it impossible for the representatives of the other parties of the National Front, controlled by the bourgeoisie, which had numerical superiority in the decisive organs endowed with power, to isolate the Communists and to stop the revolution. Thus it (the pressure . . .; Tr.) made up for the numerical weakness of the revolutionary representatives of the workers' class in these organs and enhanced their strength. *This experience, that pressure "from below" is absolutely essential for the undisturbed unfolding of the socialist revolution, is also reflected, in full measure in the theory about the possibility of the revolutionary utilization of parliament in connection with the road to socialism.*

The combination of the pressure "from above" with that "from below" — the path toward the progressive, undisturbed breaking of the resistance of the bourgeoisie, toward the gradual limitation and making impossible of a show of force by the bourgeoisie. *The real possibility of the revolutionary utilization of parliament for the road to socialism lies, therefore, in the combined mass strength of the revolutionary acting people supporting parliament as a revolutionarily active assembly which fights for the systematic fulfillment of the demands of the working people.* This coordination of actions by the broad popular masses and the revolutionary forces in parliament, in the government and in the local organs of power, mutually germinates their strength, drives the revolution ahead and infuses it with attacking and penetrating power.

The Decisive Force

Referring to Engels' idea that as the workers' class gains the support of the masses, of the working peasantry and of other exploited sections, it will become "the decisive force, to which all the other forces will have to submit willy-nilly."

Confiscation of Private Land

In accordance with the Kosice government program, the first big transfer of land was effected in people's democratic Czechoslovakia. 2,946,395 ha [hectares] of land belonging to big holders, enemies and traitors was confiscated and allotted, on the basis of decrees, to 305,148 families of agricultural workers, tenants and small-holders, and put partly under the administration of the cooperatives, national committees and the state. This land reform resulted in the almost complete liquidation of big holdings of land in the border regions, but the central parts of the country were affected by these decrees to only an insignificant measure. Big landowners, holding above 50 ha of land, and the Church still retained some 1,400,000 ha of agricultural land, which means almost a fifth of the entire land. An economically and numerically strong section of kulaks still represented a very important force of the bourgeoisie in the countryside and the bourgeoisie was still most influential with the medium farmers as well.

The possibility of a further successful advance of the revolution depended on the reinforcement of the influence of the workers' class and of the CPCS in the countryside, on a further strengthening and widening of the bond between the workers' class and the working peasantry. The road for this was the struggle for further demands of the peasants (especially the still unquenched thirst for land), a more intensive campaign for uncovering the face of the bourgeoisie and further subversion of the biggest bastion of the bourgeoisie in the countryside — the landholders' ownership of the land.

In the summer of 1946, the Communists began the fight for handing over more land to the working peasantry. They demanded a revision of the land reform of 1919, which the bourgeoisie had carried out in the pre-Munich republic. The revision affected a total of 1,027,529 ha of land and its materialization would mean the complete liquidation of the group of big landowners with over 150 ha of arable or 250 ha of agricultural land, the group of the so-called "rest-estate holders" and land speculators.

The acceptance of the demand for a revision was bound to affect severely the big landowners and the countryside bourgeoisie and, by this, the bourgeoisie as a whole. A sharp class fight with the bourgeoisie developed over the acceptance of this law.

Pressure From Above Triggers Pressure From Below
The pressure "from above" exerted by the Ministry of Agriculture, triggered a strong pressure "from below." The peasants discussed the draft proposals of the law at their meetings and their overwhelming majority demanded its acceptance.

Liquidation of Private Property
To increase the effectiveness of the pressure "from above" and "from below" against the bourgeoisie, the Communists proclaimed (on behalf of the Ministry of Agriculture) additional far-reaching demands for the working peasantry, the so-called "Hradec Program." Its basic demand was the division into lots of all big estates of over 50 ha and the complete liquidation of land held for the purpose of investment [lit.: speculation; Tr.]

The struggle for the revision of the first land reform entered the next, decisive stage. In the summer the proposal of the law was debated by Parliament. The Communists used these debates for uncovering the bourgeois leadership of the National Socialist, the Popular and the Democratic parties, and proved them to be furious defenders of the land owners and enemies of the working peasantry. Every attempt of the bourgeoisie at thwarting, delaying or limiting the proposed law was brought out into the open by the Communists in Parliament and pilloried.

The Communist pressure in the government and in Parliament (the pressure "from above") engendered more and more decisively the pressure "from below."

On July 11, the pressure from "above" and from "below" closed like the claws of a pair of pincers. The bourgeoisie, whose political positions were perceptibly shaken, had to give way. The bill on revision of the first agricultural reform was passed by the Parliament.

The consequences of this victory were: the liquidation of more of the economic positions of the bourgeoisie in the village, a big political defeat of the bourgeoisie (its increasing isolation), a considerable strengthening and broadening of the bond between the workers' class and the working peasantry. The peasants recognized that, given direct political, organizational and material help of the workers' class, they could lead a successful fight against their arch-enemy, the landowner and his helpers. Increasingly wider masses of peasants were coming over to Party positions and supported its political line aiming at further deepening of the revolution.

Industry Nationalized

By a similar method, the claws of the pincers were being closed by pressure from "above" and from "below" in the years 1945-1948, penetrating deeper and deeper into the flesh of the bourgeoisie. Thus, when the liquidation of the political and economicpositions of the occupiers and of the treacherous native grand-bourgeoisie was completed in the course of the national and democratic revolution on the basis of the Kosice program, further groups of the bourgeoisie were gradually annihilated as the revolution progressed. The nationalization in October 1945 liquidated particularly the economic power of the financial bourgeoisie, the group of industrialists dominating until then the key industries and the basic sources of raw material and the group of factory owners employing over 500 employees.

All these class clashes with the bourgeoisie had far-reaching political consequences. The influence and strength of the bourgeoisie was collapsing; the broad masses gathered with growing resolution around the CPCS and its policy.

Undermining Political Opposition

At the end of 1947 and the beginning of 1948, the progress of the class struggles confirmed that the CPCS would gain in the forthcoming elections a decisive majority and would achieve the fulfillment of its other demands with the help of a democratically manifested will of the people. It demanded the liquidation of all private capitalist enterprises employing over 50 people, a total liquidation of the group of local and foreign merchants and a total liquidation of landowners owning over 50 hectares of land.

Thus, the situation of the bourgeoisie was, at the beginning of 1948 on the eve of the new parliamentary elections, substantially different from that in 1946. While prior to the elections in 1946 the bourgeoisie had a relatively strong mass basis, the short time of less than two years of people's democratic development had been sufficient for the disintegration of the political army upon which it could formerly count. The broad masses of the people, especially working peasants, lost their illusions as regards the bourgeoisie and went over to the side of the workers' class in order to place the bourgeoisie and its anti-popular and treacherous policy into the right light in the eyes of our nations.

In 1948, when the decisive fight between the workers' class and the bourgeoisie drew closer, the bourgeoisie had only a shade of the power and influence that it used to have in 1945.

After five days of government crisis, the people settled their accounts with bourgeoisie reaction, legally and constitutionally (under consistent use of all forms of pressure from "above" and from "below").

The Revolution Consolidates Political Power

The representatives of the bourgeoisie and their agents were replaced in the government, absolutely legally and in accordance with the constitution valid since pre-Munich days (1920), by new representatives faithful to the people, selected from the ranks of the reconstituted National Front and recognizing the leading role of the Communists in the state; the government was nominated by the President of the Republic and was unanimously approved by *Parliament.*

A spontaneous and very valuable opinion of an important bourgeois émigré, the former chief of the office of the President of the Republic Jaromir Smutny:

Yes. "The irony of world history puts everything upside down. With us 'revolutionaries' and 'rebels' legal methods agree much more than illegal ones or than a coup. The parties of order, as they call themselves, die by the legal state which they created." (F. Engels, foreword to Marx' work "Class struggles in France," K. Marx — F. Engels: Selected Works, volume 1, 1950, p. 133)

In the fight for the direct national, democratic, peaceful, economic and social demands of the people, by a combined pressure from "above" and from "below," the position of the bourgeoisie in the organs of power and in the state apparatus may be weakened, step by step, and so may its economic positions, and thus the workers class heading the popular masses may be given, step by step, conditions more favorable for its fight for socialism. (Naturally, these demands will always be founded upon the concrete situation prevailing in the country concerned and will greatly differ. For example, defense of national interests by cancellation of all agreements and treaties with the United States of America damaging to the interests of the nation; prohibition of all war propaganda, punishment of warmongers and active support of the policy of collective security; abolition of all forms of racial, religious and national discrimination; fight against the monopolies, and their nationalization; carrying out of a land reform; introduction of a general system of social security; abolition of every kind of economic, social and legal inequality of women; separation of Church and state; etc.) In the course of the fight for these national, social, economic and political demands of broad masses of the working people, the following may and must be carried out successfully: a broadly founded democratization and reorganization of the organs of power (for instance, the principle that all the organs of state power, from top to bottom, are elected by the people; *the abolition of the senate and concentration of all power in the hands of the parliament;* a democratization and reorganization of the state apparatus — courts, police, army, etc.). This broad democratization is carried out, in principle, by the gradual destruction of the bourgeois state apparatus and its transformation into an instrument and source of power of the new democratic might.

All these measures and their consequences (a systematic strengthening of the positions of power of the workers' class and the gradual weakening and destruction of the economic-political supports of the bourgeoisie) are, in their entirety, the actual way toward a limitation and perhaps exclusion of any violence of the bourgeoisie against the people and thus toward prevention of civil war.

Progress toward socialism may take, under these circumstances, a democratic and constitutional course. The parliament, which will be an active revolutionary assembly relying upon the revolutionary mass movement of the workers' class and its allies, will turn into an instrument of the workers' class on its way to power, into an instrument of the transformation of the whole state and its machinery. Under these circumstances, all the changes which, in their entirety, represent a revolutionary transformation of capitalist society into a socialist one will proceed absolutely legally. The parliament may pass, in a democratic and legal way and in the name of the nation, a new constitution codifying and making possible a socialist transformation of the country.

Thus, progress toward socialism is a real possibility. Therefore, the 20th Congress of the Soviet Communist Party proclaimed with absolute frankness: *"There can be no doubt that for a number of capitalist countries a violent downthrow of the bourgeois dictatorship and, with it, a connected vehement acceleration of the class struggle is inevitable."*

Thus, the 20th Congress of the Soviet CP proclaims, in full harmony with the spirit of Marxism-Leninism, that at the present historical stage in the development of society, the possibility, of breaking the resistance of the bourgeoisie against socialist transformation of the society by non-violent means, without recourse to revolutionary violence, has matured or will mature in many countries.

Parliament: "A new instrument of socialist revolution"
Conflict between the revolutionary use of parliament and the reformist meaning of a "parliamentary way to socialism"
A revolutionary usefulness of the parliament will demand in new historical conditions, a realization of a new form of transition to the

dictatorship of the proletariat; parliament must become a new instrument of socialist revolution depriving the bourgeoisie of its power, of its means of production and materializing the building of socialism with the working class directing the policy making. The reformist "parliamentary way to socialism" denies the necessity of a revolutionary transition of capitalist to socialist society, denies the necessity of a socialist revolution, denies the necessity (under the slogan of "parliamentary democracy") of seizure of all power by the workers' class, denies the necessity of acquiring the political direction of the state and of establishing the dictatorship of the proletariat. The reformist "parliamentary way" cannot ever lead to the building up of socialism; is not, in its substance, a socialist program. It is capable of attacking within the framework of capitalism, with varying force, the consequences of capitalist exploitation but is not capable of grasping its causes, of smashing capitalism and materializing a revolutionary transformation of society.

The substance of the tactic of revolutionary use of the parliament is fully based upon the old principle of revolutionary activity of the workers class in a bourgeois parliament, worked out in detail by the classics of Marxism-Leninism and further developed in the new conditions. It starts from the following principle: Parliament in bourgeois countries is a product of historical development and cannot be erased from life. It is necessary, therefore, to work in it and to use it in the fight against bourgeois society.

In the same way as the revolutionary tactic of making use of the parliament corresponds to the revolutionary aims of the Marxist-Leninist party, the tactic of reformist use of parliament corresponds to the reformist aims of rejection of revolution.

To the reformists, parliament (an instrument of the bourgeoisie for strengthening and maintaining capitalist power) is an organ for cooperation between the workers' class and the bourgeoisie. Partial reforms achieved in the parliament (in agreement with the capitalists) serve the reformists as evidence that peaceful coexistence of bourgeoisie and the workers' class is possible, that class struggle is dying down, that revolution is superfluous and political domination of the workers' class unnecessary. Instead of the necessity of a proletarian democracy, they sustain the illusion of a parliamentary, pure democracy.

The Socialist "Labour" Parties
In many countries the reformists won the majority, often absolute majority. Their governments were in existence, and have been in existence, for extended periods of time. One of the chief propagandists of this way, the British Labour Party, already has three times had an opportunity to turn its "theories" into practice. It held the government in 1924, in the years 1929 through 1931, and for six years in 1945 through 1951.

There could be no clearer evidence of the absurdity of the idea that socialism may be built in cooperation with capitalism, without bringing down the political might of the bourgeoisie, without the dictatorship of the proletariat.

...In spite of its absolute hopelessness the theory of "a parliamentary way to socialism" is still alive in the capitalist states and appeals to the backward part of the working class and especially to the petty bourgeoisie.

Opportunist ideology and practice are a serious obstacle to the creation of a broad and revolutionary movement of the masses fighting consistently for democratic and socialist demands.

Accelerating the Communist Revolution
In the complicated class conditions of the years 1945-1948, when the question of power in people's democratic Czechoslovakia was not yet definitely settled and when power was still shared by the workers' party and the bourgeoisie, two basic political lines were opposing each other. One was the revolutionary workers' class, which had as its purpose and aim the achievement of a gradual isolation of the bourgeoisie and the closing of the ranks of the nation around the workers' class and its vanguard, the Communist Party. Its aim was consolidating the people's democracy into a state of the dictatorship of the proletariat. The second was the line of the bourgeoisie whose aim was to isolate the workers' class and its vanguard, the CPCS, to halt the national and democratic revolution and to attain with the help of Western imperialists the restoration of the capitalist domination under a dictatorship of the bourgeoisie.

In this tug-of-war situation, when the class struggle was accelerating, the workers' class fighting for complete political power was attacked from the rear by the reformist ideology and practice of the "democratic way to socialism" as preached by the right wing of the Social Democratic Party. While the workers' class under the leadership of the Communists was locked in battle with the bourgeoisie for a deeper and broader hegemony among all classes of working people, a battle for the strengthening and consolidation of its leading role in the nation, the reformists came forward with their theories denying the leading role of the proletariat and proclaiming its merging with (and thus absorption by) the other classes, for instance, with the peasantry.

This is a clear example of revision of the Marxist theory of classes. "The nation is not composed of one occupation or class and it is to its benefit that all occupational and class interests be harmonized, for an excessive elevation or attenuation of one class must necessarily mark a detriment for the other classes and thus for the whole whose gain must be our only aim." ("Lidova Demokracie," 10.6.45.)

The "Democratic Way to Socialism"
It is as if this transparent wishful thinking were the father of the theory of a permanent peaceful coexistence of capitalism and socialism in one state, of the merging of antagonistic classes. "To us, nationalization or socialization of key positions in production and distribution and protection of private ownership of small and medium production units, and especially of private ownership of small and medium agricultural property, are an expression of a wise and economical organization. . . The materialization of this plan will lead to gradual elimination of class conflict in human society." ("Draft proclamation ...," page 566.)

Within the framework of this "democratic way to socialism," obstinately supported by the right wing of the Social Democratic Party, the private capitalist production sector was to be preserved permanently and so was the bourgeoisie with its still powerful economic foundation. Also permanently to be preserved was its position of strength, used to the dissipation of the country's economy

47

and for political discrimination against the workers' class heading the state.

Also, the old reformist understanding of the role of parliament manifested itself under the influence of the right wing of social democracy, both in theory and practice, in the years 1945-1948 and was in crass conflict with the revolutionary line of using the parliament followed by the Communists.

This characteristic may be supplemented by an example demonstrating how the theory and practice of Social Democratic isolation of parliament from the revolutionary struggle of the masses of working people suited the bourgeoisie. When, in the fall of 1945, the bourgeoisie opposed the decree nationalizing key and heavy industries, the CPCS decided to appeal to the people. A gigantic mass movement for nationalization ensued, pressing the bourgeoisie with its back against the wall. The bourgeoisie, afraid of the pressure of the popular masses, proclaimed: "We consider any pressure demanding an accelerated approval of the decree to be harmful. The government needs nothing more than peace and time . . . ." ("Lidova Demokracie," 26.9.45.)

The pressure of the people's masses holding the bourgeoisie in its pincers was to be relaxed. The Social Democratic Minister of Industry, Lausman, attempted at the decisive moment to frustrate the political activity of the working people. "Folks, have patience, the draft decree on nationalization of big industry has 46 paragraphs and we are arguing the first." ("Pravo Lidu," 24.9.45)

From Capitalism to Socialism Through Democracy
In order that the reformist "democratic way" to socialism be complete, there had to be, of course, a denial of the basic condition of the possibility of victory for socialism — of the dictatorship of the proletariat. "Our state has decided for socialization in the democratic manner, that is to say, through the ballot and not through revolution and dictatorship." ("Minutes of the 20th congress of the Social Democratic Party," page 161.) Thus, solving the problems of transition from capitalism to socialism, of breaking the desperate resistance of the bourgeoisie, of expropriating the exploiters and transforming small private capitalist production into socialist production on a large scale, should be possible without the direction

48

of policy by the workers' class, without the dictatorship of the proletariat — just by phrases about some kind of pure democracy; in other words, revision and denial of the basic maxim of Marxist-Leninist theory of classes and class struggle.

The reformist theory and practice of the "parliamentary way," remained what it has always been, a theory and practice of the defense of the bourgeoisie. Its aim was the undermining of the leading role of the working class in the revolution, instead of a necessity of a proletarian democracy it nurtured illusions of "pure democracy." Therefore, it was necessary to fight systematically against the destructiveness of reformism subservient to the bourgeoisie. This warning experience convincingly points to one of the basic conditions of a revolutionary use of Parliament for the purpose of transition to socialism; namely, to the necessity of "decisive rejection of opportunist elements unable to drop the policy of compromise with the capitalists and landowners." (20th congress of the Soviet CP, "Nova Mysl," February 1956, p. 23.)

Therefore, if the workers' class is to create under its leadership a united revolutionary popular movement able to break the resistance of the reactionary bourgeois forces, it must fight systematically and energetically against reformism with its treacherous ideology and practice. Therefore, it is the duty of the workers' class to continue and step up its criticism of the reformists who, cannot and do not want to use the parliament in the fight against the capitalists and refuse to mobilize, organize and utilize the people's masses against the counter-revolutionary bourgeoisie.

The struggle for the preservation of national independence, democracy, peace and the betterment of the social position of the working people presents itself, under present conditions, increasingly as a common task of Communist and all other political parties and organizations which acknowledge the principles of socialism and democracy. In the present situation, not the questions of fundamental differences should be emphasized but those questions which are common and which reflect immediate interests.

Evidence of the possibility and success of such a struggle is again to be found in our own experience. In the course of the fight against the occupiers and their helpers among the big bourgeoisie in this country, in the course of the fight for the recovery of national and state independence and of the anti-fascist fight for democratic right of the people, a broad National Front of workers, peasants, tradesmen, intelligentsia and part of bourgeoisie was created. This National Front, headed by the workers' class, represented a decisive internal force ensuring the victory of the national and democratic revolution.

The Creation of a Socialist Bloc

The unity of action of the workers' class and the strong influence of the ideas of socialism, manifesting itself in the course of the national and democratic revolution, made it possible to conclude, in June 1945, within the framework of the National Front, a "socialist bloc." The existence of the "socialist bloc," whose representatives were in the majority in government, could signify the possibility of a relatively fast transition to socialism while a continuous strengthening of left and truly socialist elements in the non-Communist parties was proceeding. ..the main significance of the agreement was the fact that this agreement, concluded before the eyes of rank-and-file members of the parties concerned, strengthened the unity of the workers' class and made it more difficult for the bourgeoisie and its agents in the leadership of the National Socialist and Social Democratic parties to find a way out of the obligation to execute the government program which had become the political foundation of the bloc. (It fulfilled the tactical principle of obtaining from all unreliable allies concessions, obligations and promises as far-reaching as possible, this being the surest way to compromise them and to help the faithful allies within these parties. This device and this form of cooperation may lead in another situation in other countries to a gradual rapprochement between the socialist parties and this to far greater and deeper consequences.) Both these agreements and this cooperation were effected only because they came into being under the pressure of the unity of popular masses, their actual cooperation from "below."

The whole course of the struggle in the years 1945-1948 demonstrated that the decisive and basic factor in creating and strengthening the action unity of the workers' class is its creation from "below" in the course of the fight for immediate political, economic and social demands of the working people. Thus, for instance, when in 1947 the Communists put forward in the government the demand of a "Millionaires' Levy" for the benefit of the peasants suffering through the consequences of a catastrophic drought, even the representatives of the Social Democratic Party raised their voice against this demand. The Communists immediately organized a common stand and pressure by the popular masses, especially a common and resolute stand of the workers' class, for the approval of this demand. "Rude Pravo," the central organ of the CPCS, published immediately after the refusal to approve the "Millionaires' Levy" the names of all the ministers who voted against the measure and added the following disclosure: "All these gentlemen were elected by our people in the honest belief that they have subscribed to the program of the National Front. However, by their attitude, they demonstrated to the broad masses of workers, peasants, office workers and tradesmen who elected them that they protect millionaires, speculators, industrialists, landowners and merchants. There are only 35,000 such people in our country. Their votes would hardly suffice for two mandates. In fact, they found supporters in the four parties of the National Front in the government." ("Rude Pravo," 4.10.57.)

This comprehensive and clear demand of the Communists brought the rank and file members of the Social Democratic Party into the common fight against the right wing forces in their own party: Organizations as a whole stood resolutely behind the common actions. This represented a very strong pressure on the leadership of the Social Democratic Party, a weakening of the right wing and strengthening of the left, with the result that after a week's struggle, on September 11, an agreement was concluded between the leadership of the CPCS and the leadership of the Social Democratic party on common action. This agreement contained very important obligations on both sides:

1. to submit a common draft proposal for the "Millionaires' Levy";
2. to proceed jointly in the question of remuneration of state employees;
3. to fight for the unity of the National Front and to appeal to the membership of both
 parties to act in unity from "below."

51

From Democracy, to Socialism, to Marxism

This whole tactic offers a clear example of the decisive influence of unity at the bottom upon the possibility of effective cooperation with the leadership of other socialist parties.

Our experience with the creation of an action unity of the workers' class, one of the fundamental conditions of a peaceful transition to socialism, shows that the center of its true beginning must be pressure from below, systematic uncovering of the reformist theory and of cooperation with the bourgeoisie, a common fight of the broad masses of all socialist parties or parties and organizations approving the revolutionary demands of the working people; in other words, direct actions from below based on our own experience of fighting and winning.

The Soviet Model

Apart from this, the practical experience of the Czechoslovak way to socialism confirmed the validity of many basic experiences of the Great October Revolution. ...our revolution has taken its course and follows basically the way taken by the Soviet Union.

Our example has shown that Czechoslovakia's transition to the building of socialism was successful only because it was under the political direction of the workers class headed by the Marxist-Leninist Czechoslovak Communist Party. It confirmed the validity of Lenin's maxim saying that every nation advancing towards socialism "will add something specific to any existing form of democracy, to any existing form of dictatorship of the proletariat, to any concrete pace of socialist transformation of the various aspects of social life." (Lenin's Works, CS edition 1957, page 71.)

...the tasks and the form of the dictatorship of the proletariat in people's democratic Czechoslovakia correspond to the actual historical situation in Czechoslovakia. This form of the dictatorship of the proletariat differs by a number of points from the form adopted by the October Socialist Revolution:

• By the existence of the National Front as a political expression of unity between the workers' class and the working peasantry and the other working people;

• By the existence of more political parties within the framework of the National Front. These non-Communist political parties are, in their substance, petty-bourgeois parties, fully recognizing, however, and subordinating themselves to, the leadership of the CPCS and serving the building of socialism and the common fight of the people for peace;

• By the recognition of former bourgeois parliamentary institutions, such as the parliament, president, etc., which have, however, adopted a new, socialist purpose;

• By not depriving the bourgeoisie of the right to vote, having adopted the principle of universal, secret and direct ballot. Our way has supplied a definite proof that Marxism-Leninism has nothing in common with a "cult of violence" and has shaken very seriously the lying propaganda of reformism, attempting to persuade the working masses that the basic difference between the revolutionary workers' movement and reformism lies in the question of a "non-bloody" way to socialism.

Also, a "cult of violence" cannot be followed by the workers' class, because a violent armed fight is not at all advantageous to it from the point of view of its aim — the achievement of a complete socialist revolution. This aim combines two inseparable tasks: to oust the power of the bourgeoisie and to organize a new, higher method of social production, to organize and build socialism.

The Czechoslovak example is evidence that an apparently slower progress of socialist revolution (by gradual transition of national and democratic revolution into a socialist revolution) was actually the faster way, because the two-in-one task of the socialist revolution began to be fulfilled simultaneously. While fast removal of the consequences of war, efforts to renew quickly production forces, economic progress of the country, a new working discipline, advance of education and culture, were at first aimed at the total political defeat of the bourgeoisie, all these efforts, in their consequence, created simultaneously the main conditions of a faster and more definite securing of power in the hands of the working class. In February 1948, i.e., at the time when the workers' class had already achieved all political power and when the people's democracy was realized as a state of the dictatorship of the proletariat,

(a) the state apparatus was already in existence in principle and the working class could use it in its fight for socialism;

(b) the first important successes had already been achieved in creating a new working discipline and a new relationship to work;

(c) the working masses had already gained experience in state, organizational and educational work;

(d) new forms of organization of working people were in existence, as required for leading the broad popular masses in socialist building; these new forms represented an important part of the system of the dictatorship of the proletariat following a complete assumption of power by the working class;

(e) the economy of the country, disrupted by the war, was already rehabilitated in principle.

All this is created and achieved by the proletariat only after its victory, if violent attainment of socialism through civil war must be chosen. This is truly convincing evidence that a "cult of violence" is absolutely unacceptable for Marxist-Leninist parties because it is in conflict with their fundamental needs and aims. The confirmation of this principle by the actual course of our revolution has greatly enhanced the attraction of socialism.

The Czech Example: Building Proletarian Internationalism
In appraising our experiences and our contribution to the international workers' movement this must not be forgotten. The possibility of the peaceful progress of socialist revolution making revolutionary use of the parliament, as pointed our by the 20th Congress of the Soviet CP, is a product of new class conditions created by far-reaching objective and subjective changes in the world. It is a product of class consequences resulting from the existence of the world socialist system and its political, economic and ideological strength.

About Robert Welch University Press ...
This new edition of *And Not A Shot Is Fired* is an edifying successor to *Philip Dru:Administrator* — the premier book-length publication of Robert Welch University Press. In the Foreword to *Philip Dru*, journalist William Norman Grigg described that novel (written by Woodrow Wilson's "alter ego," Edward Mandell House) as being an essential part of any political science student's collection of "political works which are read primarily for precautionary reasons."

Though published as a work of fiction in 1912, *Philip Dru* served as a clear blueprint for the heinous "isms" of the middle part of this century that drew the world into two world wars, and coerced a substantial portion of the earth's population into living under totalitarian collectivism.

And Not A Shot Is Fired is a case study of the effects of such machinations on a single country — Czechoslovakia. Thomas R. Eddlem notes in its Foreword: "This document is a 'how-to' manual for totalitarian takeover of an elected parliamentary system of government through mainly legal and constitutional means." Kozak and his coconspirators manipulated the Czechoslovak people into voting themselves into slavery by using what he called "pressure from above" and "pressure from below."

But why should a busy modern American set aside the time to read this brief history of an extinct state? The reason is that the same tactics described in Kozak's book are in wide use today, by other conspirators. As former Czechoslovakian Vice-Premier Petr Zenkl warned: "Read it and heed it, gentlemen of the Free World, while you are free."

The administrators of RWU Press do not take lightly the responsibility of making revealing studies of this caliber readily available to all students, instructors, and devotees of political science and public affairs. (Or at least to those sufficiently inspired to approach these studies from a perspective of true intellectual fervor, curiosity and, we would hope, a commitment to improve the human condition.)

In selecting titles for publication, the editors of RWU Press shall be guided by a philosophy of respect for intellectual, historical, and ethical truth — rather than by the current trend of "political correctness." For the former is perennial, the latter is transitory.

"There is one thing a professor can be absolutely certain of," noted University of Chicago professor Allan Bloom in *The Closing of the American Mind,* "almost every student entering the university believes, or says he believes, that truth is relative.... The relativity of truth is not a theoretical insight but a moral postulate, the condition of a free society, or so they see it. They have all been equipped with this framework early on, and it is the modern replacement for the inalienable natural rights that used to be the traditional American grounds for a free society.... Openness used to be the virtue that permitted us to seek the good by using reason. It now means accepting everything and denying reason's power." It is "not a means to exploring different answers to the great questions, but an excuse not to try to answer them at all."

Robert Welch University Press will not flee from its self-assigned mission to explore "different answers to the great questions."

The most pressing question of all, in the context of American society on the eve of the Twenty-first Century, is: How can we preserve, defend, and export America's greatest commodity: a legacy of political freedom in which all other freedoms — cultural, religious, economic, and academic — will flourish?

Now, a step back in time to 1913 and into the 1920's in United States. Let's call it the...

Growth of Communism in the United States

In 1974, a book titled *Wall Street and the Bolshevik Revolution* was written by Anthony C. Sutton. This is something to which you should pay particular attention in that the data comes directly from declassified government documents from 1918 to the early 1920's.

Sutton says the bankers weren't driven by Bolshevik zeal but by the desire for capital gain. Considering the power in the financial world of the men described in his book, I wouldn't have been so charitable.

For the sake of saving time, I'm taking many details directly from a .pdf version of the book.

As you connect the names, dates, and places, you'll see the plan unfold for the Bolshevik takeover of Russia with the financial support of the western free world. Little did the bankers of that era know of the political demon they would be unleashing on the world in which we live today. Or did they? The entire scheme is a gigantic money-laundering project to support communism in the Soviet Union.

One of the most interesting items of data in *Wall Street and the Bolshevik Revolution* was the fact that most of the offending bankers were located at 120 Broadway, NYC, NY.

The following is from **Chapter VIII**:

William B. Thompson, who was in Petrograd from July until November last, has made a personal contribution of $1,000,000 to the Bolsheviki for the purpose of spreading their doctrine in Germany and Austria ....
Washington Post, February 2, 1918

While collecting material for this book a single location and address in the Wall Street area came to the fore — 120 Broadway, New York City. Conceivably, this book could have been written incorporating only persons, firms, and organizations located at 120 Broadway in the year 1917. Although this research method would have been forced and unnatural, it would have excluded only a relatively small segment of the story.

Author's note: The material relating to William B. Thompson was retained for this quote only to show how much he supported the Bolshevik Revolution. His name will be mentioned again as the text progresses.

This quotation will give you an idea of the close physical proximity of the players in this game.

The building at 120 Broadway was in 1917 known as the Equitable Life Building...it occupies a one-block area at Broadway and Pine, and has thirty-four floors. The Bankers Club was located on the thirty-fourth floor. The tenant list in 1917 in effect reflected American involvement in the Bolshevik Revolution and its aftermath. For example, the headquarters of the No. 2 District of the Federal Reserve System — the New York area — by far the most important of the Federal Reserve districts, was located at 120 Broadway. The offices of several individual directors of the Federal Reserve Bank of New York and, most important, the American International Corporation were also at 120 Broadway. By way of contrast, Ludwig Martens, appointed by the Soviets as the first Bolshevik "ambassador" to the United States and head of the Soviet Bureau, was in 1917 the vice president of Weinberg & Posner — and also had offices at 120 Broadway.*

The author then makes an observation which is as true today as it was when the book was published in 1974. I quote: "With an almost unanimous lack of perception, the academic world has described and analyzed international political relations in the context of an unrelenting conflict between capitalism and communism, and rigid adherence to this Marxian formula has distorted modern history."

Frankly, it's beyond me how Sutton could have made such a comment. The academic world is filled with communists who call themselves progressives. Occasionally, one will have the courage to reveal his true character, but it's rare. In his *Communist Manifesto*, Marx made clear the purpose of the movement could not be declared for what it was because it wouldn't succeed. My point is this...the world of academia is full of leftists (communists). Why would they tattle on themselves?

After the McCarthy hearings of the late 1940s to the mid-1950s, most of the communists went underground into the media and the world of academia although the colleges had been infested with Bolshivist professors since about 1914. More on that later.

Senator Joseph McCarthy (The Senate Internal Security Subcommittee) and Representative Richard Nixon (House Unamerican Activities Committee) peeled back the veil of duplicity and complicity that was going on in the entertainment world (the Hollywood Ten), our State Department, and our nuclear defense program by exposing Alger Hiss, Julius and Ethel Rosenberg, and Robert Oppenheimer. All were convicted of being traitors in one degree or another. The Rosenbergs were executed while Hiss and Oppenheimer spent many years in prison.

Now, back to 120 Broadway, NYC...

Take a look at the following list of directors of the American International Corporation and you'll see an interlocking of corporate and banking power that was more than formidable. This data is quoted directly from Sutton's book. You'll recognize several names.

The directors of American International and some of their associations were (in 1917):

J. OGDEN ARMOUR Meatpacker, of Armour & Company, Chicago; director of the National City Bank of New York, and mentioned by A. A. Heller in connection with the Soviet Bureau (see p. 119).

GEORGE JOHNSON BALDWIN Of Stone & Webster, 120 Broadway.

During World War I Baldwin was chairman of the board of American International Shipbuilding, senior vice president of American International Corporation, director of G. Amsinck (Von Pavenstedt of Amsinck was a German espionage paymaster in the U.S., see page 65), and a trustee of the Carnegie Foundation, which financed the Marburg Plan for international socialism to be controlled behind the scenes by world finance (see page 174-6).

C. A. COFFIN Chairman of General Electric (executive office: 120 Broadway), chairman of- cooperation committee of the American Red Cross.

W. E. COREY (14 Wall Street) Director of American Bank Note Company, Mechanics and Metals Bank, Midvale Steel and Ordnance, and International Nickel Company; later director of National City Bank.

ROBERT DOLLAR San Francisco shipping magnate, who attempted in behalf of the Soviets to import tsarist gold rubles into U.S. in 1920, in contravention of U.S. regulations.

PIERRE S. DU PONT Of the du Pont family.

PHILIP A. S. FRANKLIN Director of National City Bank.

J.P. GRACE Director of National City Bank.

R. F. HERRICK Director, New York Life Insurance; former president of the American Bankers Association; trustee of Carnegie Foundation.

OTTO H. KAHN Partner in Kuhn, Loeb. Kahn's father came to America in 1948, "having taken part in the unsuccessful German revolution of that year."

According to J. H. Thomas (British socialist, financed by the Soviets), "Otto Kahn's face is towards the light."

H. W. PRITCHETT Trustee of Carnegie Foundation.

PERCY A. ROCKEFELLER Son of John D. Rockefeller; married to Isabel, daughter of J. A. Stillman of National City Bank.

JOHN D. RYAN Director of copper-mining companies, National City Bank, and Mechanics and Metals Bank. (See frontispiece to this book.)

W. L. SAUNDERS Director the Federal Reserve Bank of New York, 120 Broadway, and chairman of Ingersoll-Rand. According to the *National Cyclopaedia* (26:81): "Throughout the war he was one of the President's most trusted advisers." See page 15 for his views on the Soviets.

J. A. STILLMAN President of National City Bank, after his father (J. Stillman, chairman of NCB) died in March 1918.

C. A. STONE Director (1920-22) of Federal Reserve Bank of New York, 120 Broadway; chairman of Stone & Webster, 120 Broadway; president (1916-23) of American International Corporation, 120 Broadway.

T. N. VAIL President of National City Bank of Troy, New York

F. A. VANDERLIP President of National City Bank.

E. S. WEBSTER Of Stone & Webster, 120 Broadway.

A. H. WIGGIN Director of Federal Reserve Bank of New York in the early 1930s.

BECKMAN WINTHROPE Director of National City Bank.

WILLIAM WOODWARD Director of Federal Reserve Bank of New York, 120 Broadway, and Hanover National Bank.

The interlock of the twenty-two directors of American International Corporation with other institutions is significant. The National City Bank had no fewer than ten directors on the board of AIC; Stillman of NCB was at that time an intermediary between the Rockefeller and Morgan interests, and both the Morgan and the Rockefeller interests were represented directly on AIC.

Kuhn, Loeb, and the du Ponts each had one director. Stone & Webster had three directors. No fewer than four directors of AIC (Saunders, Stone, Wiggin, Woodward) either were directors of or were later to join the Federal Reserve Bank of New York. We have noted in an earlier chapter that William Boyce Thompson, who contributed funds and his considerable prestige to the Bolshevik Revolution, was also a director of the Federal Reserve Bank of New York — the directorate of the FRB of New York comprised only nine members.

THE INFLUENCE OF AMERICAN INTERNATIONAL ON THE REVOLUTION

Having identified the directors of AIC, we now have to identify their revolutionary influence.

As the Bolshevik Revolution took hold in central Russia, Secretary of State Robert Lansing requested the views of American International Corporation on the policy to be pursued towards the Soviet regime. On January 16, 1918—barely two months after the takeover in Petrograd and Moscow, and before a fraction of Russia had come under Bolshevik control—-William Franklin Sands, executive secretary of American International Corporation, submitted the requested memorandum on the Russian political situation to Secretary Lansing. Sands' covering letter, headed 120 Broadway, began:

> January 16, 1918
> To the Honourable
> Secretary of State
> Washington D.C.
> Sir,
> I have the honor to enclose herewith the memorandum which you requested me to make for you on my view of the political situation in Russia.

I have separated it into three parts; an explanation of the historical causes of the Revolution, told as briefly as possible; a

61

suggestion as to policy and a recital of the various branches of American activity at work now in Russia ....[8]

Although the Bolsheviks had only precarious control in Russia — and indeed were to come near to losing even this in the spring of 1918 — Sands wrote that already (January 1918) the United States had delayed too long in recognizing "Trotzky." He added, "Whatever ground may have been lost, should be regained now, even at the cost of a slight personal triumph for Trotzky."[9]

Author's note: The following list will give you an idea of the close proximity of the bankers who supported the Bolshevik Revolution.

Firms located at, or near, 120 Broadway:
American International Corp
120 Broadway
National City Bank
55 Wall Street
Bankers Trust Co Bldg
14 Wall Street
New York Stock Exchange
13 Wall Street/12 Broad
Morgan Building corner Wall & Broad
Federal Reserve Bank of NY
120 Broadway
Equitable Building
120 Broadway
Bankers Club 120 Broadway
Simpson, Thather & Bartlett
62 Cedar St
William Boyce Thompson
14 Wall Street
Hazen, Whipple & Fuller
42nd Street Building
Chase National Bank
57 Broadway
McCann Co 61 Broadway
Stetson, Jennings & Russell
15 Broad Street
Guggenheim Exploration
120 Broadway

Weinberg & Posner
120 Broadway
Soviet Bureau 110 West
40th Street
John MacGregor Grant Co
120 Broadway
Stone & Webster
120 Broadway
General Electric Co
120 Broadway
Morris Plan of NY
120 Broadway
Sinclair Gulf Corp
120 Broadway
Guaranty Securities
120 Broadway
Guaranty Trust
140 Broadway

Author's note: Now that we have the names and locations of the players in this chess match of capitalism versus communism, let's go back to the beginning of Sutton's book and do some historical and political cherry-picking that may make you wretch.

Chapter I, "The Actors On the Revolutionary Stage" of *Wall Street and the Bolshevik Revolution* opens with the following letter:

Dear Mr. President:
I am in sympathy with the Soviet form of government as that best suited for the Russian people...

Letter to President Woodrow Wilson (October 17, 1918) from William Lawrence Saunders, chairman, Ingersoll-Rand Corp.; director, American International Corp.; and deputy chairman, Federal Reserve Bank of New York

Author's note: considering the source of the letter, which is shocking, to say the least, Sutton goes on to hypothesize—

There has been a continuing, albeit concealed, alliance between international political capitalists and international revolutionary socialists — to their mutual benefit. This alliance has gone unobserved largely because historians — with a few notable exceptions — have an unconscious Marxian bias and are thus locked into the impossibility of any such alliance existing. The open-minded reader should bear two clues in mind: monopoly capitalists are the bitter enemies of laissez-faire entrepreneurs; and, given the weaknesses of socialist central planning, the totalitarian socialist state is a perfect captive market for monopoly capitalists, if an alliance can be made with the socialist power-brokers.

Author's note: When Sutton writes of historians having an "unconscious" bias to Marxism, it's necessary to question his reasoning. Anyone who has studied the political and educational scene of the past one hundred years can see the bias is quite conscious and with malice of forethought. That's the reason our nation is at the crossroads of making a decision to embrace freedom, liberty, and capitalism, or to accept the oppression of socialism, fascism, and perhaps even communism.

Our education system has been slowly indoctrinating students, who eventually are supposed to become productive citizens, in the "benefits" of socialism since the time of John Dewey and earlier.

Dewey (1859-1952) was an important early developer of the philosophy of pragmatism and one of the founders of functional psychology. **He was a major representative of progressive education and liberalism.** *Wikipedia*

Also, Sutton mentions George Kennan's study of the Bolshevik Revolution, *Russia Leaves the War* (published 1956), and that the book maintains there was little or no relationship between the Revolution and Wall Street. A position the Overman Committee (September, 1918-June, 1919), chaired by Senator Lee Slater Overman, had proven to be false and was ignored by Kennan in his work. The Overman Committee was devoted to an investigation of Bolshevik and German political influence in the United States. It is from the work of the Overman Committee that Sutton's book was written once the data was declassified in 1970.

As an aside, you will find that George Kennan wore many hats. *Wikipedia* says he "was an American adviser, diplomat, political scientist, and historian, best known as 'the father of containment' and as a key figure in the emergence of the Cold War. He later wrote standard histories of the relations between Russia and the Western powers." He had been the U. S. ambassador to the Soviet Union 1951-1952.

As "the father of containment," Kennan theorized that it was proper to contain Soviet Communism by diplomatic strategy rather to defeat the ideology of Communism on the battlefield. Needless to say, the theory was a failure. Communism hasn't been defeated, and it can be contained only as long as the United States remains the strongest military force in the world.

In spite of President Reagan's accomplishments, communism is still trying to bury us. However, they now have considerable help from Islam and bureaucrats within our own government. Remember Washington's first farewell address?

Communism is the mortal enemy of capitalism. As a college professor of mine was wont to say—"Communism and capitalism cannot coexist."

Since he had lived with Vladimir Lenin for two weeks in October of 1917, he probably knew whereof he spoke.

The Bolshevism of Wall Street...

According to Sutton, the Bolshevism of Wall Street was fairly well known among the inner circles of the informed elite as early as 1919.

The following is an interesting quotation that caught my eye:

The financial journalist Barron recorded a conversation with oil magnate E. H. Doheny in 1919 and specifically named three prominent financiers, William Boyce Thompson, Thomas Lamont and Charles R. Crane:

Aboard S.S. Aquitania, Friday Evening, February 1, 1919.

Spent the evening with the Dohenys in their suite. Mr. Doheny said: If you believe in democracy you cannot believe in Socialism. Socialism is the poison that destroys democracy. Democracy means opportunity for all. Socialism holds out the hope that a man can quit work and be better off. Bolshevism is the true fruit of socialism and if you will read the interesting testimony before the Senate Committee about the middle of January that showed up all these pacifists and peace-makers as German sympathizers, Socialists, and Bolsheviks, you will see that a majority of the college professors in the United States are teaching socialism and Bolshevism and that fifty-two college professors were on so-called peace committees in 1914. President Eliot of Harvard is teaching Bolshevism. The worst Bolshevists in the United States are not only college professors, of whom President Wilson is one, but capitalists and the wives of capitalists and neither seem to know what they are talking about. William Boyce Thompson is teaching Bolshevism and he may yet convert Lamont of J.P. Morgan & Company. Vanderlip is a Bolshevist, so is Charles R. Crane. Many women are joining the movement and neither they, nor their husbands, know what it is, or what it leads to. Henry Ford is another and so are most of those one hundred historians Wilson took abroad with him in the foolish idea that history can teach youth proper demarcations of races, peoples, and nations geographically.[3]

Author's note: This quotation paints a picture of cooperation between capitalism and communism (euphemistically called socialism), which has been ongoing for at least one hundred years. In the 2008 general election in the U. S., the Communists came within a gnat's eyelash of winning the war. The general election of 2012 will tell us if the tide has turned in the favor of capitalism, freedom and liberty.

Leon Trotsky comes to the United States

This detail on Trotsky has been brought to your attention to show one example of the devious manner in which the Bolshevik Revolution was supported by the bankers and politicians of the U. S. through money-laundering at the highest levels of banking in the U. S., Germany, and Sweden.

You will have a revolution, a terrible revolution. What course it takes will depend much on what Mr. Rockefeller tells Mr. Hague to do. Mr. Rockefeller is a symbol of the American ruling class and Mr. Hague is a symbol of its political tools.

Leon Trotsky, in New York Times, *December 13, 1938. (Hague was a New Jersey politician).*

An introduction to Leon Trotsky (Russian: 7 November 1879 – 21 August 1940), born Lev Davidovich Bronshtein, was a Russian Marxist revolutionary and theorist, Soviet politician, and the founder and first leader of the Red Army. *Wikipedia.*

Leon Trotsky was an important character in the drama of the Bolshevik Revolution; therefore, we must learn of his background.

Trotsky was an internationalist revolutionary who was ejected from Russia, France, and Spain only to wind up in the United States in 1917.

He had started the newspaper *Pravda* (*Truth* in the English translation) in 1908. The paper was a bi-weekly socialist publication that was aimed at the Russian laborer, and was written in Vienna, Austria, where he lived and from where it was smuggled into the Soviet Union. He lived in exile in Vienna because of his disagreements with Lenin's Soviet leadership.

While in the U. S., Trotsky, who spoke only German and Russian, and worked as an electrician, somehow acquired a $10,000 bank account for which no one could account. Eventually, it was determined the money mysteriously came from Germany. This became the subject of the Senate Overman Committee one day while questioning Colonel Vladimir Hurban, the Washington attaché to the Czech delegation.

Hurban yielded very little information about the source of Trotsky's funding except for the fact he remembered it was from Germany. The committee adjourned its hearing for that day at 5:45 p.m., just before the true source of Trotsky's funds was divulged. When hearings were resumed the following day, Trotsky's money was no longer of interest to the committee. Strange, but who can account for the political minuet of politicians? You always must wonder what it is they are hiding.

According to Sutton, it was later learned the funds originated in Germany and were funneled through the German newspaper, *Volks-zeitung,* a daily journal in New York City that was subsidized by the German government.

So...we have Leon Trotsky, a Russian who also spoke German, in New York City and who had to get back to Russia to help Lenin with the Bolshevik Revolution. This is just a guess on my part, but when you have someone like Trotsky, who is a known revolutionary, in your country, and who wants to get back to his native country to participate in a revolution, you do everything you can to find an American passport for him. That'll get him out of the U. S. and off to a place where he can do no harm—unless you're a supporter of his cause. Then, the plot thickens.

Enter stage left—Woodrow Wilson, our own president, made it possible for an American passport to be issued to Trotsky.[1]

Leon Trotsky leaves the United States

At this point, please consider the following quote from Sutton's work:

> Consequently, by virtue of preferential treatment for Trotsky, when the S.S. *Kristianiafjord* left New York on March 26, 1917, Trotsky was aboard and holding a U.S. passport — and in company with other Trotskyite revolutionaries, Wall Street financiers, American Communists, and other interesting persons, few of whom had embarked for legitimate business. This mixed bag of passengers has been described by Lincoln Steffens, the American Communist:

> "The passenger list was long and mysterious. Trotsky was in the steerage with a group of revolutionaries; there was a Japanese revolutionist in my cabin. There were a lot of Dutch hurrying home from Java, the only innocent people aboard. The rest were war messengers, two from Wall Street to Germany".[12]

> Notably, Lincoln Steffens was on board en route to Russia at the specific invitation of Charles Richard Crane, a backer and a former chairman of the Democratic Party's finance committee.

> Charles Crane, vice president of the Crane Company, had organized the Westinghouse Company in Russia, was a member of the Root mission to Russia, and had made no fewer than twenty-three

visits to Russia between 1890 and 1930. Richard Crane, his son, was confidential assistant to then Secretary of State Robert Lansing. According to the former ambassador to Germany William Dodd, Crane "did much to bring on the Kerensky revolution which gave way to Communism."[13] And so Steffens' comments in his diary about conversations aboard the S.S. *Kristianiafjord* are highly pertinent:"...all agree that the revolution is in its first phase only, that it must grow. Crane and Russian radicals on the ship think we shall be in Petrograd for the re-revolution.[14]

More on Charles Crane:

In brief, the unlikely and puzzling picture that emerges is that Charles Crane, a friend and backer of Woodrow Wilson and a prominent financier and politician, had a known role in the "first" revolution and traveled to Russia in mid-1917 in company with the American Communist Lincoln Steffens, who was in touch with both Woodrow Wilson and Trotsky. The latter in turn was carrying a passport issued at the orders of Wilson and $10,000 from supposed German sources. On his return to the U.S. after the "re-revolution," Crane was granted access to official documents concerning consolidation of the Bolshevik regime: This is a pattern of interlocking — if puzzling — events that warrants further investigation and suggests, though without, at this point, providing evidence, some link between the financier Crane and the revolutionary Trotsky.

Author's note: With these pieces in place, we have the Bolshevik Revolution of October, 1917. The leaders were the Menshevik, Leon Trotsky, and the Bolshevik, Vladimir Lenin.

Are you beginning to get the feeling that Barack Hussein Obama may be the embodiment of Woodrow Wilson, Franklin Delano Roosevelt, Lyndon Baines Johnson, and Jimmy Carter on steroids?

Eventually, Trotsky and Lenin disagreed on the conduct of the government that emerged from the revolution and Trotsky went into exile in Mexico after stays in Turkey and Norway.

Trotsky lived in the Coyoacán area of Mexico City at the home (The Blue House) of the painter Diego Rivera* and Rivera's wife and fellow painter, Frida Kahlo, with whom Trotsky had an affair. His final move was a few blocks away to a residence on Avenida Viena in May 1939, following a break with Rivera. *Wikipedia*

He was assassinated in Mexico City on May 21, 1940 at the age of sixty.

*When I saw this connection between Trotsky and Rivera, it brought to mind an experience I had in 2010 with my nine year old granddaughter's social studies curriculum at the Kyrene School District's elementary school, Cerritos in Phoenix, AZ.

Apparently, during a class session, the teacher showed a video presentation of some Mexican artwork. Diego Rivera was one of the artists who was presented. When I learned of the situation, I asked the teacher if he knew of Rivera's political background. He did not. When I told him of the man's politics, he seemed to be unimpressed. It's my opinion that subliminal indoctrination has been going on for at least ninety years in our school system, at all levels, a la John Dewey. It's almost a certainty you could find several books and commentaries that would support this hypothesis if you tried. One book that immediately comes to mind is *Dumbing Down our Kids* by Charles J. Sykes. The book was published in 1995 and was well received by all but the education establishment.

The Trotsky story has been used only to show the lengths to which our financial institutions, probably backed by political strength from the White House, went to make it possible for the Bolshevik Revolution to take place.

1. from the footnotes in *Wall Street and the Bolshevik Revolution* found on page twenty-two of the online .pdf file. Reference is made to U. S. State Department Decimal File, 316-85-1002.

Now that we have those tidbits of history tucked safely away in our minds, let's summarize this...

money-laundering project...

The players are U. S. banks and corporations, German banks, and at least one Swedish bank which was led by Olof Aschberg, owner and founder of the Nya Banken in Stockholm. He was responsible for obtaining a $50 million loan for Russia through a syndicate of American bankers headed by James Stillman's National City Bank. Aschberg was in Russia in 1916 with Rolph Marsh of Guaranty Trust and Samuel MacRoberts and Charles V. Rich of National City Bank arranging loans for a Morgan-Rockefeller consortium.

According to Sutton, the loan was completed on June 5, 1916. This transaction resulted in a Russian credit of $50 million in New York at an annual rate of 7½%. Once this was done, a 150 million ruble credit was established for the NCB (National City Bank) syndicate in Russia. The New York syndicate then issued certificates in its own name at an annual rate of 6½% in the U. S. markets. Thus, a profit was made on the loan to Russia.

While all of this was transpiring, Olof Aschberg and the Nya Banken were the pipeline for funds from the German government to the Bolsheviks who would eventually overthrow the Kerensky government which was established in May, 1917. In October, 1917, Lenin's Bolsheviks overthrew the Kerensky government in a violent act by killing the members of parliament while they were in session. It was because of this horrific violence the Communist Party of Czechoslovakia developed a method of taking over a parliamentary government without firing a shot.

This is a very quick and loose summary of some unbelievably complex events in our history. In order to obtain all of the details, you'll have to read the book, *Wall Street and the Bolshevik Revolution*.

So what, you ask? That was then and this is now. Well, things haven't changed much. The Wall Street fraternity still supports the Democrat Party, which has become the party of socialism. President

Barak Hussein Obama may have tarnished his presidential image a bit with his profoundly socialistic policies and his dictatorial use of constitutional executive privilege, thereby causing some consternation in the Wall Street bunch.

Now it's time to see how the American Civil Liberties Union and the Council of Foreign Relations fit into the puzzle. It's interesting to note the proliferation of subversive activities which started under the Woodrow Wilson administration. He probably was our most liberal, progressive president until President Obama. It's difficult to say which was/is the most socialistic president?

First the ACLU

The ACLU was founded in 1920 by Roger Nash Baldwin, Crystal Eastman, and Walter Nelles. Albert DeSilver gave financial support.

American Civil Liberties Union statement of principles

From their website in June, 2012:

The ACLU is our nation's guardian of liberty, working daily in courts, legislatures and communities to defend and preserve the individual rights and liberties that the Constitution and laws of the United States guarantee everyone in this country.

These rights include:

Your First Amendment rights - freedom of speech, association and assembly; freedom of the press, and freedom of religion.
Your right to equal protection under the law - protection against unlawful discrimination.
Your right to due process - fair treatment by the government whenever the loss of your liberty or property is at stake.
Your right to privacy - freedom from unwarranted government intrusion into your personal and private affairs.

The ACLU also works to extend rights to segments of our population that have traditionally been denied their rights, including people of color; women; lesbians, gay men, bisexuals and transgender people; prisoners; and people with disabilities.

If the rights of society's most vulnerable members are denied, everybody's rights are imperiled. Support the ACLU today.

The U.S. Supreme Court had yet to uphold a single free speech claim when Roger Baldwin, Crystal Eastman, Albert DeSilver and others formed the ACLU in 1920. Activists languished in jail for distributing anti-war literature. State sanctioned violence against African Americans was routine. Women won the right to vote only in August of that year. Constitutional rights for lesbians and gays, bisexual and transgender people in those days were unthinkable.

Now, let's become familiar with the background of the principal founders of the ACLU. Following are biographical sketches of Baldwin, Eastman, and Nelles, and DeSilver. These have been taken from online sources for the sake of simplicity and, I hope, accuracy.

Note: the ACLU's founders were from families of means—not an insignificant fact, and they were also very influential among those participating in the Communist movement in the United States.

Spartacus Educational
http://www.spartacus.schoolnet.co.uk/USAbaldwinR.htm provides this brief biography of Baldwin:

Roger Nash Baldwin

Roger Nash Baldwin was born in Wellesley, Massachusetts, on 21st January, 1884. **After graduating from Harvard University in 1905**, Baldwin taught sociology at Washington University in St. Louis (1906-09).

Baldwin was a pacifist and on the outbreak of the First World War joined with Abraham Muste, Norman Thomas, Scott Nearing and Oswald Garrison Villard to form the Fellowship of Reconciliation (FOR).

Soon after the outbreak of the First World War, Baldwin, Crystal Eastman, Jane Addams, Lillian Wald, Paul U. Kellogg and Oswald Garrison Villard established the American Union Against Militarism (AUAM). Wald became the AUAM's president and Eastman its executive director. Over the next couple of years the AUAM lobbied against America's possible involvement in the war. It also campaigned against conscription, the arms trade and American imperialism in Latin America and the Caribbean. Baldwin replaced Crystal Eastman as the AUAM's executive director in 1916. The following year Baldwin, Eastman and Norman Thomas established the National Civil Liberties Bureau (NCLB).

In 1918 Baldwin was imprisoned for his public support of conscientious objectors. While in prison he met fellow radicals, Agnes Smedley and Mollie Steimer. Smedley had charged with diseminating birth control information. Steiner had been imprisoned for circulating leaflets in opposition to United States intervention in the Russian Civil War.

After his release in 1919 Baldwin joined the Industrial Workers of the World (IWW). Baldwin later recalled: "I was a member of it for a very brief period in which I tried to earn an honest living with my hands. I was experimenting with manual labor, as a preparation, I thought, for a possible role in the labor movement. I lasted about four months. I came to the conclusion that I was better suited for something else. Clarence Darrow once said that it's a lot easier to be a friend of the working man than a working man. I found that out."

In 1920 he joined with Norman Thomas, Jane Addams, Chrystal Eastman, Clarence Darrow, John Dewey, Abraham Muste, Elizabeth Gurley Flynn and Upton Sinclair to form the American Civil Liberties Union (ACLU).

Baldwin was appointed as the first director of the ACLU and over the next thirty five years was involved in the campaign against

74

the Palmer Raids, the Espionage Act, the Tennessee Anti-Evolution Law, Jim Crow, McCarthyism and Racial Segregation.

Roger Nash Baldwin died on 26th August, 1981.

If you ever doubted the man's politics, here are two quotations that will explain his intentions.

Roger Nash Baldwin Quotes

I am for socialism, disarmament, and, ultimately, for abolishing the state itself... I seek the social ownership of property, the abolition of the propertied class, and the sole control of those who produce wealth. Communism is the goal. — Harvard Classbook of 1935

This one is damning if anything ever was...

Do steer away from making it look like a Socialist enterprise…We want also to look like patriots in everything we do. **We want to get a good lot of flags, talk a good deal about the Constitution and what our forefathers wanted to make of this country, and to show that we are really the folks that really stand for the spirit of our institutions."**-Baldwin's advice in 1917 to Louis Lochner of the socialist People's Council in Minnesota. -

Regarding Crystal Eastman, I'm again using Spartacus Educational for biographical data. There is quite a lot of material here, but I wanted you to see what gave her the principles she followed. Therefore, a few of her commentaries have been included. This is done because it appears this woman had a lot of influence in the politics of the U. S. at the time—influences that have carried over into the policies of today. Emphasis in bold type is mine.

Crystal Eastman

Crystal Eastman was born in Marlborough, Massachusetts, on 25th June, 1881. **Both her parents**, Samuel Eastman and Annis Ford, **were church ministers**. Her brother, Max Eastman, was born two years later. He later wrote: "She was beautiful and socially disarming, and yet inwardly a mighty girl, as we named her in the bosom of the family... The qualities in Crystal that I most rejoiced in were her ruthless sincerity and logic; the inexhaustible fountain of understanding love that made these qualities bearable; a supervening humor…a gift of entering into the problems of other people as though she had no problems of her own - a veritable genius for friendship and wise counsel; and withal a passionate joy in the adventure of living her own life."

In 1889 her mother was one of the first women to be ordained as a minister. Crystal recalled: "When my mother preached we hated to miss it. There was never a moment of anxiety or concern; she had that secret of perfect platform ease which takes all strain out of the audience. Her voice was music; she spoke simply, without effort, almost without gestures, standing very still. And what she said seemed to come straight from her heart to yours. Her sermons grew out other own moral and spiritual struggles. For she had a stormy, troubled soul, capable of black cruelty and then again of the deepest generosities. She was humble, honest, striving, always beginning again to try to be good."

Crystal Eastman **graduated from Vassar College in 1903. She also obtained a degree in sociology at Columbia University (1904) and her law degree at New York City University Law School (1907).** Claude McKay met her during this period: "The moment I saw her and heard her voice I liked Crystal Eastman. I think she was the most beautiful white woman I ever knew. She was of the heavy or solid type of female, and her beauty was not so much other features... but in her magnificent presence. Her form was something after the pattern of a splendid draft horse and she had a way of holding her head like a large bird poised in a listening attitude."

Eastman settled in Greenwich Village and joined a community of feminists that included Inez Milholland, Mary Heaton Vorse, Doris Stevens, Susan Glaspell, Neith Boyce, Madeleine Doty, and Ida Rauth. In 1907 Paul U. Kellogg, editor of the social work magazine, *Charities and the Commons*, hired her to investigate labour conditions for the Russell Sage Foundation's Pittsburgh Survey. Over the next year Eastman carried out the first in-depth sociological investigation of industrial accidents ever undertaken. Other members of the team included Lewis Hine, Elizabeth Beardsley Butler, John R. Commons, John A. Fitch and Joseph Stella.

In June 1909 Charles E. Hughes, the Governor of New York, appointed Eastman to become the first woman member of the Employer's Liability Commission. In this role she drafted New York State's first worker's compensation law and in 1910 she published her book Work Accidents and the Law.

Eastman married Wallace Benedict in 1911. The couple moved to Milwaukee but the marriage was not a success and ended in divorce. Eastman reputation as a political campaigner grew and in 1913 she became investigating attorney for the U.S. Commission on Industrial Relations. Later that year Eastman was a delegate to the Seventh Congress of the International Woman Suffrage Alliance in Budapest. During the conference Eastman met Aletta Jacobs (Holland), Emmeline Pethick-Lawrence (England) and Rosika Schwimmer (Hungary).

In 1913 Eastman joined with Alice Paul, Lucy Burns, Mabel Vernon, Olympia Brown, Mary Ritter Beard, Belle LaFollette, Doris Stevens, Helen Keller, Maria Montessori and Dorothy Day to form the Congressional Union for Women Suffrage (CUWS) and attempted to introduce the militant methods used by the Women's Social and Political Union in Britain. This included organizing huge demonstrations and the daily picketing of the White House. Over the next couple of years the police arrested nearly 500 women for loitering and 168 were jailed for "obstructing traffic".

As a pacifist Eastman was a strong opponent of the First World War. Soon after the outbreak of the conflict Eastman, Jane Addams, Lillian Wald, Paul U. Kellogg and Oswald Garrison Villard established the American Union Against Militarism (AUAM). Wald became the AUAM's president and Eastman its executive director. Over the next couple of years the AUAM lobbied against America's possible involvement in the war. It also campaigned against conscription, the a   rms trade and American imperialism in Latin America and the Caribbean.

On the 10th January, 1915, Eastman joined over 3,000 women at a meeting in the ballroom of the New Willard Hotel in Washington and formed the Woman's Peace Party. Jane Addams was elected chairman and other women involved in the organization included Mary McDowell, Florence Kelley, Alice Hamilton, Anna Howard Shaw, Belle La Follette, Fanny Garrison Villard, Emily Balch, Jeanette Rankin, Lillian Wald, Edith Abbott, Grace Abbott, Mary Heaton Vorse, Charlotte Perkins Gilman, Carrie Chapman Catt, Freda Kirchwey, Emily Bach, and Sophonisba Breckinridge.

In 1916, Eastman married British poet and fellow anti-war activist, Walter Fuller. In the same year, she invited her friend Roger Baldwin to run the American Union Against Militarism office while she took a brief leave to give birth to her first child. *The following year Eastman joined Baldwin, Norman Thomas, Albert DeSilver and Clarence Darrow to establish the National Civil Liberties Bureau (NCLB).* (Emphasis is mine.)

Crystal worked with her brother, Max Eastman, on the radical journal The Masses. After it was closed down by the authorities because of its opposition to American involvement in the First World War, they joined with Art Young and Floyd Dell to establish the The Liberator. In the first edition it was stated: "The Liberator will be owned and published by its editors, who will be free in its pages to say what they truly think. It will fight in the struggle of labor. It will fight for the ownership and control of industry by the workers, and will present vivid and accurate news of the labor and socialist movements in all parts of the world." The journal published information about socialist movements throughout the world and was the first to break the news that the Allies had invaded Russia.

After the war, Woodrow Wilson appointed A. Mitchell Palmer as his attorney general. Worried by the revolution that had taken place in Russia, Palmer became convinced that Communist agents were planning to overthrow the American government. Palmer recruited John Edgar Hoover as his special assistant and together they used the Espionage Act (1917) and the Sedition Act (1918) to launch a campaign against radicals and left-wing organizations.

A. Mitchell Palmer claimed that Communist agents from Russia were planning to overthrow the American government. On 7th November, 1919, the second anniversary of the Russian Revolution, over 10,000 suspected communists and anarchists were arrested in what became known as the Palmer Raids. Palmer and Hoover found no evidence of a proposed revolution but large number of these suspects were held without trial for a long time. The vast majority were eventually released but Emma Goldman and 247 other people, were deported to Russia.

In January, 1920, another 6,000 were arrested and held without trial. Palmer and Hoover found no evidence of a proposed revolution but large number of these suspects, many of them members of the Industrial Workers of the World (IWW), continued to be held without trial. When Palmer announced that the communist revolution was likely to take place on 1st May, mass panic took place. In New York, five elected Socialists were expelled from the legislature.

Concerned by these events Eastman joined with **Roger Baldwin, Norman Thomas,** Jane Addams, Florence Kelley, Lillian Wald, **Felix Frankfurter (later a Supreme Court justice,**) Oswald Garrison Villard, Paul Kellogg, **Clarence Darrow, John Dewey**, Charles Beard, Abraham Muste, **Elizabeth Gurley Flynn and Upton Sinclair** to form the American Civil Liberties Union (ACLU).

The ACLU's main concern was to defend the civil rights that were guaranteed in state and federal constitutions. This included:

(1) First Amendment rights: These include freedom of speech, association and assembly, freedom of the press, and freedom of religion, including the strict separation between church and state.

(2) Equal protection of the law: The right to equal treatment regardless of race, sex, religion, national origin, sexual orientation, age, physical handicap, or other such classification.

(3) Due process of law: The right to be treated fairly when facing criminal charges or other serious accusations that can result in such penalties as loss of employment, exclusion from school, denial of housing, or cut-off of benefits.

(4) The right of privacy and autonomy which cannot be penetrated by the government or by other institutions, like employers, with substantial influence over the individual's rights.

In December 1920, Crystal Eastman wrote in *The Liberator*: "Many feminists are socialists, many are communists, not a few are active leaders in these movements. But the true feminist, no matter how far to the left she may be in the revolutionary movement, sees the woman's battle as distinct in its objects and different in its methods from the workers' battle for industrial freedom. She knows, of course, that the vast majority of women as well as men are without property, and are of necessity bread and butter slaves under a system of society which allows the very sources of life to be privately owned by a few, and she counts herself a loyal soldier in the working-class army that is marching to overthrow that system. But as a feminist she also knows that the whole of woman's slavery is not summed up in the profit system, nor her complete emancipation assured by the downfall of capitalism.

In 1922 *The Liberator* was taken over by Robert Minor and the Communist Party. Eastman now wrote for The Nation and Equal Rights, a journal established by Alice Paul. Blacklisted for her left-wing political opinions and unable to find work, Eastman and her husband Walter Fuller moved to London. While in England she worked fot the Daily Herald and Time and Tide, a feminist journal established by Lady Margaret Rhondda. She also took part in the campaign to get votes for women on the same terms as men.

Walter Fuller died of a stroke in September 1927. Eastman returned home but was in poor health and died of a brain hemorrhage on 8th July, 1928. An obituary by Freda Kirchwey in *The Nation* pointed out that: "In her short life Crystal Eastman brushed against many other lives, and wherever she moved she carried with her the breath of courage and a contagious belief in the coming triumph of freedom and decent human relations. These were her religion. Her strength, her beauty, her vitality and enthusiasm, her rich and compelling personality - these she threw with reckless vigor into every cause that promised a finer life to the world." As another friend wrote at the time: "She was for thousands a symbol of what the free woman might be."

(1) Crystal Eastman wrote about her childhood in an article in *The Nation* (16th March, 1927)

When my mother preached we hated to miss it. There was never a moment of anxiety or concern; she had that secret of perfect platform ease which takes all strain out of the audience. Her voice was music; she spoke simply, without effort, almost without gestures, standing very still. And what she said seemed to come straight from her heart to yours. Her sermons grew out other own moral and spiritual struggles. For she had a stormy, troubled soul, capable of black cruelty and then again of the deepest generosities. She was humble, honest, striving, always beginning again to try to be good.

With all her other interests she was thoroughly domestic. We children loved her cooking as much as we loved her preaching. And she was all kinds of devoted mother, the kind that tucks you in at night and reads you a story, and the kind that drags you to the dentist to have your teeth straightened. But I must leave her now and try to fill out the picture. My father, too, played a large part in my life. He was a generous man, the kind of man that was a suffragist from the day he first heard of a woman who wanted to vote.

From the moment he knew that my mother wanted to preach, he helped and encouraged her. Without his coaching and without his local prestige, it is doubtful if she could have been ordained. And my father stood by me in the same way, from the time when I wanted to cut off my hair and go barefoot to the time when I began to study law. When I insisted that the boys must make their beds if I had to make mine, he stood by me. When I said that if there was dishwashing to be done they should take their turn, he stood by me.

81

And when I declared that there was no such thing in our family as boys' work and girls' work, and that I must be allowed to do my share of wood-chopping and outdoor chores, he took me seriously and let me try.

Once when I was twelve and very tall, a deputation of ladies from her church called on my mother and gently suggested that my skirts ought to be longer. My mother, who was not without consciousness of the neighbors' opinions, thought she must do something. But my father said, "No, let her wear them short. She likes to run, and she can't run so well in long skirts

A few years later it was a question of bathing suits. In our summer community I was a ringleader in the rebellion against skirts and stockings for swimming. On one hot Sunday morning the other fathers waited on my father and asked him to use his influence with me. I don't know what he said to them but he never said a word to me. He was, I know, startled and embarrassed to see his only daughter in a man's bathing suit with bare brown legs for all the world to see. I think it shocked him to his dying day. But he himself had been a swimmer; he knew he would not want to swim in a skirt and stockings. Why then should I?

(2) Statement issued by the Crystal Eastman, Roger Baldwin and Norman Thomas for the Civil Liberties Bureau (2nd July 1917)

It is the tendency even of the most 'democratic' of governments embarked upon the most 'idealistic of wars' to sacrifice everything for complete military efficiency. To combat this tendency where it threatens free speech, free press, freedom of assembly and freedom of conscience - the essentials of liberty and the heritage of all past wars worth fighting - that is the first function of the AUAM today. To maintain something over here that will be worth coming back to when the weary war is over.

(3) Crystal Eastman, *Birth Control Review* (January, 1918)

Whether other feminists would agree with me that the economic is the fundamental aspect of feminism, I don't know. But on this we are surely agreed, that Birth Control is an elementary essential in all aspects of feminism. Whether we are the special followers of Alice

Paul, or Ruth Law, or Ellen Key, or Olive Schreiner, we must all be followers of Margaret Sanger. Feminists are not nuns. That should be established. We want to love and to be loved, and most of us want children, one or two at least. But we want our love to be joyous and free - not clouded with ignorance and fear. And we want our children to be deliberately, eagerly called into being, when we are at our best, not crowded upon us in times of poverty and weakness. We want this precious sex knowledge not just for ourselves, the conscious feminists; we want it for all the millions of unconscious feminists that swarm the earth, - we want it for all women.

(4) *The Liberator*, editorial, introductory issue (March, 1918)

Never was the moment more auspicious to issue a great magazine of liberty. With the Russian people in the lead, the world is entering upon the experiment of industrial and real democracy. Inspired by Russia, the German people are muttering a revolt that will go farther than its dearest advocates among the Allies dream. The working people of France, of Italy, of England, too, are determined that the end of autocracy in Germany shall be the end of wage-slavery at home. America has extended her hand to the Russians. She will follow in their path. The world is in the rapids. The possibilities of change in this day are beyond all imagination. We must unite our hands and voices to make the end of this war the beginning of an age of freedom and happiness for mankind undreamed by those whose 'minds comprehend only political and military events. With this ideal The Liberator comes into being on Lincoln's Birthday February 12, 1918.

The Liberator will be owned and published by its editors, who will be free in its pages to say what they truly think. It will fight in the struggle of labor. It will fight for the ownership and control of industry by the workers, and will present vivid and accurate news of the labor and socialist movements in all parts of the world.

It will advocate the opening of the land to the people, and urge the immediate taking over by the people of railroads, mines, telegraph and telephone systems, and all public utilities.

It will stand for the complete independence of women - political, social and economic - and an enrichment of the existence of mankind.

It will stand for a revolution in the whole spirit and method of dealing with crime.

It will join all wise men in trying to substitute for our rigid scholastic kind of educational system one which has a vivid relation to life.

It will assert the social and political equality of the black and white races, oppose every kind of racial discrimination, and conduct a remorseless publicity campaign against lynch law.

It will oppose laws preventing the spread of scientific knowledge about birth control.

(7) Crystal Eastman, Now We Can Begin (December, 1920)

The problem of women's freedom is how to arrange the world so that women can be human beings, with a chance to exercise their infinitely varied gifts in infinitely ways, instead of being destined by the accident of their sex to one field of activity - housework and child-raising. And second, if and when they choose housework and child-raising to have that occupation recognized by the world as work, requiring a definite economic reward and not merely entitling the performer to be dependent on some man...

(10) Crystal Eastman, *Daily Herald* (May, 1925)

In all countries where women have won the vote Suffragists tend to separate into two distinct groups so far as their public activities go: there are the humanitarians who devote themselves to securing those measures of general human betterment for which enlightened women have always stood, and there are the feminists, who, as long as any inequality exists between men and women, regard it as the chief object of organised women to remove it.

Already in the United States the line is clearly drawn, and the two groups are organised. There is the Woman's Party, which exists solely "to remove all forms of the subjection of women," and the League of Women Voters, which takes up child welfare, education, social hygiene, international co-operation to prevent war, etc., as well as uniform laws concerning women.

Elsewhere the same division will inevitably take place; women who have worked side by side to win the vote will divide according to whether their interests are mainly humanitarian or mainly feminist. Sometimes the two groups find themselves directly antagonistic, as for instance in the matter of special labour restrictions for women.

The feminists oppose such restrictions, when they apply to women and not to men, as an unwarranted interference with woman's freedom and as a serious handicap in competition with men. The humanitarians defend them as a necessary protection to motherhood and the race.

A lively debate on this subject took place at the recent International Congress of Women at Rome, in connection with the resolution that "no special regulations for women's work, different from regulations for men, should be imposed contrary to the wishes of the women concerned.

Walter Nelles

From *Wikipedia:*

Walter Nelles (1883 – 1937) was an American lawyer and law professor. Nelles is best remembered as the first chief legal counsel of the National Civil Liberties Bureau and its successor, the American Civil Liberties Union. In this connection, Nelles achieved public notice for his legal work on behalf of pacifists charged with violating the Espionage Act during World War I and in other politically charged civil rights and constitutional law cases in later years.

Early years

 Walter Nelles was born April 21, 1883 in Leavenworth, Kansas, the son of a civil engineer.[1] **Nelles attended the prestigious Phillips Exeter Academy in Exeter, New Hampshire in preparation for an Ivy League collegiate education.[1] Upon graduation from Exeter, Nelles enrolled in Harvard University, from which he graduated in 1905 with a Bachelors degree.[1]**

 After graduation, Nelles taught as an instructor at the University of Wisconsin from the fall of 1905 to the spring of 1907.[1] Nelles then left Madison to **return to Harvard, receiving a Masters degree in 1908 before moving on Harvard Law School.[1] He graduated from Harvard Law with an LL.B. in 1911.**[1] During the period of his graduate education, Nelles also taught as an instructor at Lowell Institute and Radcliffe College.[1]

Career

 After passing the bar examination, Nelles entered private legal practice.

 Holding pacifist beliefs himself,[2] following the entry of the United States into World War I in April 1917 Nelles was persuaded by his old college classmate Roger Baldwin to leave his practice to become house counsel for the fledgling National Civil Liberties Bureau (NCLB) of the American Union Against Militarism that Baldwin had helped launch.[3] This organization, based in New York City, would eventually emerge as the American Civil Liberties Union.

 The Civil Liberties Bureau in its first years dealt primarily with cases involving conscientious objectors and political opponents of the war who faced charges under the so-called Espionage Act. Among those high-profile cases which Nelles handled included the trial of the American Socialist Society and its Rand School of Social Science and the trial of Max Eastman and his publication, The Masses.[1]

 The offices of the National Civil Liberties Bureau were raided by the Department of Justice on August 30, 1918 by agents who seized all of Nelles' files.[4] The raid was based upon invalid search warrants.

Nelles and Baldwin were joined in the main office of the National Civil Liberties Bureau by Albert DeSilver, a lawyer who left private practice to work full time on the defense of civil liberties in the courts.[5] The troika guided the activities of the NCLB and the successor ACLU in its earliest years. Roger Baldwin later fondly recalled their partnership:

"We made a team which was never after equalled in the American Civil LIberties Union. DeSilver contributed the quick unerring judgment, with a gay and easy approach to tough problems; Nelles, the reflective opinions of a studious lawyer sometimes aroused by hot indignations; and I, the techniques of the social case worker, an organizer and a publicity man for such limited publicity as was open to us."[6]

The three men "loved each other," Lucille B. Milner, secretary of the NCLB remembered.[6] The team was abruptly shattered when DeSilver was killed in a fall from a railroad car in 1924, dying at the age of 36.[7] Nelles later memorialized his fallen colleague by writing his biography, published by W.W. Norton & Co. in 1940.[8]

In 1920, Nelles served on the defense team of the five Socialist members of the New York State Assembly who were denied the right to assume the seats to which they had been elected by the Republican Speaker of the House Thaddeus C. Sweet, working in concert with members of both the Republican and Democratic Parties.[1]

The liberal Nelles also sought to mediate sectarian fighting among American radicals, sitting with Roger Baldwin and others on a special committee established in August 1922 to investigate charges levied by Abraham Cahan and the Jewish Daily Forward that the Friends of Soviet Russia (FSR) organization was engaged in the misappropriation of funds raised for the relief of famine in Soviet Russia.[9] The committee ultimately exonerated the FSR of these charges, but Nelles declined to sign the final report owing to the appointment of a law partner as counsel for that organization — a circumstance which thereby created a potential conflict of interest.[9]

Throughout the 1920s, Nelles participated in a loose partnership of left wing attorneys, including Joseph Brodsky, Swinburne Hale, Carol Weiss King, and Isaac Shorr.[10]

Academic career

Nelles served on the faculty of Yale Law School where he often taught courses on the history of labor injunctions.

Politics

Nelles was a social democrat and a member of the League for Industrial Democracy during the 1920s.[1] At the time of his death he was regarded by friends as a liberal rather than a socialist.[2]

Albert DeSilver

From *Wikipedia*:

Albert DeSilver (August 27, 1888-December 7, 1924)[1] was a founding member of the American Civil Liberties Union (ACLU).

DeSilver **graduated from Yale** in 1910, where he was a member of Skull and Bones,[1] and then **earned a law degree at Columbia Law School (1913) (editor Columbia Law Review)**. Though he was being groomed for a place in New York's legal establishment, he resigned his law practice in 1918 to become one of the founding members of the National Civil Liberties Bureau (later known as the American Civil Liberties Union) in order to devote himself full-time to defending conscientious objectors, other citizens, and immigrants against unconstitutional persecution under new laws such as the Espionage Act of 1917 and the Sedition Act of 1918. During World War I, DeSilver used his own war bonds to post bail for defendants in free speech cases.

At the founding of the ACLU in 1920, DeSilver was named Associate Director and worked in legal defense, public education, and lobbying. While alive, **DeSilver provided more than half of the ACLU's operating funds on an annual basis.** He was killed by an express train at age 36.[1] After his death, DeSilver's wife Margaret continued contributing to the ACLU each year in his name.

Footnotes

1.^ a b c "Obituary Record of Graduates of Yale University Deceased during the Year 1924-1925". Yale University. 1925. pp. 1442–1443.

Author's note: As I put together the foregoing biographies, a common thread emerged—all of the founders were from Ivy League colleges and universities. Baldwin was a Harvard grad, as was Nelles. Eastman was a graduate of Vassar and Columbia University Law School while DeSilver was a graduate of Yale. Although, Vassar could be the exception since it was open only to women at that time, but was considered one of the elite colleges for women, as were Bryn Mawr, Radcliffe, and Barnard.

All but Baldwin were lawyers.

Eastman's parents were both ministers.

Interestingly enough, Norman Thomas had a similar background. His father was a Presbyterian minister. Also, you'll find that his alma mater was Princeton University, another Ivy League school.

Since Thomas was affiliated with the ACLU, let's take a look at his biography.

Norman Thomas

Spartacus Educational

Norman Thomas, the son of a Presbyterian minister, was born in Marion, Ohio, on 20th November, 1884. **He studied political science under Woodrow Wilson at Princeton University and graduated in 1905.**

In 1905, Thomas helped to establish the Intercollegiate Socialist Society. Other members included Jack London, Upton Sinclair,

Clarence Darrow (a graduate of Dartmouth College, another Ivy League institution), Florence Kelley, Anna Strunsky, Bertram D. Wolfe, Jay Lovestone, Rose Pastor Stokes and J.G. Phelps Stokes. Its stated purpose was to "throw light on the world-wide movement of industrial democracy known as socialism."

Thomas did voluntary social work in New York City before studying theology at the Union Theological Seminary. Influenced by the writings of the Christian Socialist movement in Britain, Thomas became a committed socialist. Thomas was ordained in 1911 and became pastor of the East Harlem Presbyterian Church.

A pacifist, Thomas believed that the First World War was an "immoral, senseless struggle among rival imperialisms". His brother shared his views and went to prison for resisting the draft. Thomas joined with Abraham Muste, Scott Nearing and Oswald Garrison Villard to form the Fellowship of Reconciliation (FOR). In 1917 Thomas, Crystal Eastman and Roger Baldwin established the National Civil Liberties Bureau (NCLB).

In 1918 he founded and edited the *World Tomorrow* and two years later joined with Jane Addams, Elizabeth Gurley Flynn and Upton Sinclair to establish the American Civil Liberties Union. As well as being associate editor of *The Nation* (1921-22), he was co-director of the League of Industrial Democracy (1922-37), an organization he had created with Jack London and Upton Sinclair. Thomas was also a frequent contributor to its journal, *The Unemployed* (1930-32).

Thomas, a member of the Socialist Party, was its candidate for Governor of New York in 1924. After the death of Eugene Debs, Thomas became the party's presidential candidate in 1928, 1932 and 1936. Although easily defeated, **Thomas had the satisfaction of seeing Franklin D. Roosevelt introduce several measures that he had advocated during his presidential campaigns.**

Thomas joined Burton K. Wheeler and Charles A. Lindbergh in forming the America First Committee (AFC) in September 1940 and soon became the most powerful isolationist group in the United States. The AFC had four main principles: (1) The United States must build an impregnable defense for America; (2) No foreign power, nor group of powers, can successfully attack a prepared America; (3) American democracy can be preserved only by keeping out of the European War; (4) "Aid short of war" weakens national defense at home and threatens to involve America in war abroad.

The AFC influenced public opinion through publications and speeches and within a year had over 800,000 members. The AFC was dissolved four days after the Japanese Air Force attacked Pearl Harbor on 7th December, 1941. Although previously a pacifist, Thomas now supported United States involvement in the Second World War. However, he was critical of some aspects of Roosevelt's policies, including the internment of Japanese Americans and big business control of war production.

Thomas was the Socialist Party presidential candidate in 1940, 1944 and 1948. A strong critic of the Soviet communism, Thomas also denounced rearmament and the development of the Cold War. Other issues associated with Thomas during the post-war period included his campaigns against poverty, racism and the Vietnam War.

Thomas wrote several books on politics, including *Is Conscience a Crime?* (1927), *As I See It* (1932), *A Socialist Faith* (1951), *The Test of Freedom* (1954), *The Prerequisites of Peace* (1959) and *Socialism Re-examined* (1963).

Norman Thomas died on 19th December, 1968.

Note: Some of his commentaries have been included in order to give you an idea how his mind worked.

(1) Norman Thomas, *New Republic* (26th May 1917)

As conscientious objectors we turn to your journal because, more powerfully than any other, it has expressed in subtle analyses our abiding faith in humane wisdom. You have never countenanced the evil doctrine of the brute coercion of the human will. You have preached and practised the virtue of tolerance, the kind of tolerance for the lack of which the state grows mechanized and conscienceless.

You know something of the machinery of unfair play. You understand the tyranny of sham shibboleths. You appreciate the menace of military psychology. We appeal to you, strategically situated as you are, to assist the cause of the conscientious objectors. We beg you to note the following facts:

In the evolution of the human mind we discover a gradually widening hiatus between physical competence and intellectual moral competence. So deeply imbedded in our life values is this distinction that we feel rather ashamed of being too expert physically. The man of blood and iron does not appeal to our finer perceptions as a being altogether worthy of our worshipful attention. (The God whom we worship is neither a jingo nor a militarist.) But Voltaire - he of the skinny shanks and the anemic face - what exuberant pride wells up in the greatest and in the least of us at the sound of that marvelous name! And soft-spoken Jesus - what fitting tribute can the reeling world lay at the feet of him who died that goodwill and loving kindness might assuage the hearts of inimical men.

The complexity and richness of life have permitted, and increasingly so, the more or less free play of all modes of energy. There are many men best adapted by training and temperament to the performance of physical acts of heroism; there are some men more naturally suited to the performance of intellectual deeds of courage, while yet some others shine in deeds of moral bravery.

Why sanction the inhuman device of forcing all manner of men into the narrowly specific kind of devotion for which so many of them are hopelessly unfit? Tolerance arises from the existence of varying types of doers, all willing to respect one another's special competence. It is not too extreme to assert that in wartime (as in peacetime) some of the most heroic deeds are performed by those who do not (and, if called upon, would not) take up arms in defense of the cause. There are other forms of bravery than the purely military one. Let us be reasonable.

The one ineradicable fact which no amount of official intimidation can pulverize out of existence is that there is a type of man to whom (military) participation in war is tantamount to committing murder. He cannot, he will not commit murder. There is no human power on God's earth that can coerce him into committing (what he knows to be) the act of murder. You may call him sentimentalist, fool, slacker, mollycoddle, woman - anything "disreputable" you please. But there he is, a tremendous fact. Shall he be maltreated for his scruples? Or shall he be respected (as his denders are) for his conscientiousness? We cannot leave so momentous an issue to chance or to the cold machinery of administration. Men of sensitive insight must help prepare a social setting within America sufficiently hospitable to all conscientious objectors.

It is good to remind ourselves of our instinctive respect for conscientious objectors. When a man is called to serve on a jury empaneled in a murder case, he may be honorably excused from duty if he has conscientious objections to the death penalty. When we think sanely we are not averse to honoring the man of conscience provided he be an active friend of mankind and not a mere ease-taker. The test of manhood lies in service; not in one particular kind of service (suitable to one particular type of mind and body) but genuine service genuinely rendered to humanity.

Hence the philosophic value of tolerance. To keep alive genuine tolerance in wartime is the greatest single achievement to which rationalists can dedicate themselves. America is caught in this insidious entanglement; obsessed with the tradition - the mere outward form and symbol - of liberty of conscience, she has failed to realize the living need of a real grant and a substantial practice of our vaunted freedom of conscience. It is not the tradition we lack; only a vital belief in that tradition.

In times of precarious peace, when the social classes wage an almost relentless warfare and the daily grind of poverty and distress lays armies of the proletariat low, life for the disadvantaged groups is made more or less livable only by the thought that between them and their official superiors certain constitutional and humane guarantees of tolerance exist as safeguards of mutual understanding. There is room for difference of opinion. There is a breathing space for discussion.

How desperate must the social situation have become if large numbers of conscientious and law-abiding citizens have begun to feel an appalling sense of uneasiness in the presence of huge inscrutable forces, far beyond their power of control or sympathetic understanding. Why this amazing disquietude? The answer is simple and straightforward. There is no longer the sense - so natural and dear to free men - of being able to appeal from manifestly unfair decisions. Too many subordinate officials are being vested with a tremendous authority over impotent human beings.

(2) Statement issued by the Norman Thomas, Roger Baldwin and Crystal Eastman for the Civil Liberties Bureau (2nd July 1917)

It is the tendency even of the most 'democratic' of governments embarked upon the most 'idealistic of wars' to sacrifice everything for complete military efficiency. To combat this tendency where it threatens free speech, free press, freedom of assembly and freedom of conscience - the essentials of liberty and the heritage of all past wars worth fighting - that is the first function of the AUAM today. To maintain something over here that will be worth coming back to when the weary war is over.

(3) Norman Thomas, *The Profit System and Unemployment, The Unemployed* (December, 1930)

Power driven machinery makes it possible to support great populations in plenty. It has changed the basis of our civilization from one of enforced frugality to abundance. In spite of its mismanagement it has shortened hours and in many cases lightened the burden of monotonous and back-breaking toil. Yet under the the profit system the story of the progress of machinery is literally written in tears and blood. And for every advance step in technological progress the under dog has paid in the loss of his job.

This is true because we have never asked: how can we use machinery to provide more abundant goods and increase leisure for everybody? Instead the profit seeking owners of factories have said: how can we increase profits? It is easy to how that in the long run machinery by making it possible to have more things makes possible more jobs as well as shorter hours of labor. But men eat in the short run, and in the short run the boss introduces a new machine in the hope of making an immediately greater profit, which profit is very often realized only by cutting down his payroll. The employer who does this is not a villain. Under the profit system his business is to make profit. He can't help it if that means giving some men the bitter leisure of unemployment and speeding up others.

Only planned production for use, the abolition of parasitic ownership and the increase of spending power in the hands of the masses of the workers will end unemployment. I do not say that this way to end unemployment is easy. In the long run it will have to take account of the whole world and not merely just the United States. The final answer to unemployment and to poverty is intelligent international Socialism. There is no other way. Immediate remedies for some of the suffering of unemployment will be good not only in themselves but because they help our progress toward this goal.

(4) In March 1942 Freda Kirchwey, editor of *The Nation* argued that the fascist press should be banned in the United States. In a letter to Kirchwey, Norman Thomas objected to this point of view (3rd April, 1942)

It is a rather terrible thing that liberals should now be the spokesmen for a jittery program which, if it means anything, can only be interpreted to mean no criticism of the Administration except from us. In ten years or less it won't be the people you want to suppress now who will be suppressed and stay suppressed by your theory; it will be yourselves along with many others, unless, indeed, you want to go farther than I think you do in support of a Roosevelt totalitarianism. Don't forget that neither Roosevelt nor anybody else is immortal. The principles once established are apt to outlive men.

(5) John Gates, The Story of an American Communist (1959)

A few people, including Mrs. Roosevelt, Norman Thomas and A. J. Muste, did support amnesty for us. These particular personalities had been staunch defenders of civil liberties throughout the years. But even here something bothered me. If any people were justified in not coming to our defense, it was just these three whom I have named. Had we not heaped personal and political abuse upon them (alternating with periods of praise)? I asked myself how we would have responded had the situation been reversed, and my answer was not a comforting one. I came to feel that these individuals must have a moral superiority over us, that there must be something decidedly wrong with the attitude of communism toward democracy.

(6) Fenner Brockway, *Towards Tomorrow* (1977)

Norman Thomas, succeeding a hero of my youth, Eugene Debs, was Socialist candidate for the Presidency during one of my visits. I met him many times and through the years we remained friends. He was originally a minister of religion and still had the appearance of one, tall, silver-haired, clean-shaven, domed forehead, a distinguished scholarly figure. I found he was respected throughout America by members of all Parties. I remember at a football match the spectators round me discussed the election whilst waiting for the game to begin. "Thomas is the best of the three, but he's got no chance. I'm voting Roosevelt," said a man, and I was impressed by the many who agreed. Thomas had a continuously developing mind. On my first visit he was a typical Social Democrat of the Centre, except that he was a pacifist. On my third visit he had moved far to the Left. He was a pioneer in denouncing America's part in the Vietnam War.

Now for an analysis of the...

Council on Foreign Relations

As before, liberal use is made of the *Wikipedia* material. As you review the data, you'll see a few remarks made for emphasis or clarity. Wikipedia is used because the material fits with everything I've learned about the CFR since 1964. The accuracy of the information can be accepted as generally factual. Please note the year of inception. This is at the end of Wilson's administration.

From *Wikipedia*:
Not to be confused with Committee on Foreign Relations.

CFR Headquarters located in the former Harold Pratt House in New York City

Abbreviation: CFR

Formation: 1921

Type: Public policy think tank

Headquarters: 58 East 68th Street

Location: New York City and Washington, D.C.

President: Richard N. Haass

Website: www.cfr.org

The Council on Foreign Relations (CFR) is an American nonprofit, nonpartisan membership organization, publisher, and think tank specializing in U.S. foreign policy and international affairs. Founded in 1921 and headquartered at 58 East 68th Street in New York City, with an additional office in Washington, D.C., **the CFR is considered to be the nation's "most influential foreign-policy think tank".[1] It publishes a bi-monthly journal,** ***Foreign Affairs.***

Mission

As stated on its website, the CFR's mission is to be "a resource for its members, government officials, business executives, journalists, educators and students, civic and religious leaders, and other interested citizens in order to help them better understand the world and the foreign policy choices facing the United States and other countries."

The CFR aims to maintain a diverse membership, including special programs to promote interest and develop expertise in the next generation of foreign policy leaders. It convenes meetings at which government officials, global leaders and prominent members of the foreign policy community discuss major international issues. **Its think tank, the David Rockefeller Studies Program, is composed of about fifty adjunct and full-time scholars, as well as ten in-resident recipients of year-long fellowships, who cover the major regions and significant issues shaping today's international agenda. These scholars contribute to the foreign policy debate by making recommendations to the presidential administration, testifying before Congress, serving as a resource to the**

diplomatic community, interacting with the media, authoring books, reports, articles, and op-eds on foreign policy issues.

The council publishes *Foreign Affairs*, "the preeminent journal of international affairs and U.S. foreign policy." It also publishes *Independent Task Forces* which bring together experts with diverse backgrounds and expertise to work together to produce reports offering both findings and policy prescriptions on important foreign policy topics. To date, the CFR has sponsored more than fifty reports.[2]

The CFR aims to provide up-to-date information and analysis about world events and U.S. foreign policy. In 2008, CFR.org's "Crisis Guide: Darfur" was awarded an Emmy Award by the Television Academy of Arts and Sciences, in the category of "New Approaches to News & Documentary Programming: Current News Coverage." In 2009, the Crisis Guide franchise won another Emmy for its "Crisis Guide: The Global Economy," in the category of business and financial reporting.

Early history *(This is really interesting when you consider the schools represented by the scholars. Several of them are from Ivy League institutions of learning.)*

The earliest origin of the Council stemmed from a working fellowship of about 150 scholars called "The Inquiry" tasked to brief President Woodrow Wilson about options for the postwar world when Germany was defeated. Through 1917–1918, this academic band, including Wilson's closest adviser and long-time friend "Colonel" Edward M. House, as well as Walter Lippmann, gathered at 155th Street and Broadway at the Harold Pratt House in New York City, to assemble the strategy for the postwar world. The team produced more than 2,000 documents detailing and analyzing the political, economic, and social facts globally that would be helpful for Wilson in the peace talks. Their reports formed the basis for the Fourteen Points, which outlined Wilson's strategy for peace after war's end.[3]

These scholars then traveled to the Paris Peace Conference, 1919, that would end the war; it was at one of the meetings of a small group of British and American diplomats and scholars, on May 30, 1919, at the Hotel Majestic, that both the Council and its British counterpart, the Chatham House in London, were born.[4]

Some of the participants at that meeting, apart from Edward House, were Paul Warburg, Herbert Hoover, Harold Temperley, Lionel Curtis, Lord Eustace Percy, Christian Herter, and **American academic historians James Thomson Shotwell of Columbia University, Archibald Cary Coolidge of Harvard, and Charles Seymour of Yale.**

In 1938 they created various Committees on Foreign Relations throughout the country. These later became governed by the American Committees on Foreign Relations in Washington, D.C.

The Council on Foreign Relations, a sister organization to the Royal Institute of International Affairs in London (commonly known as Chatham House), was formed in 1922 as a noncommercial, nonpolitical organization supporting American foreign relations.[5] From its inception the Council was bipartisan, welcoming members of both Democratic and Republican parties. It also welcomed Jews and African Americans, although women were initially barred from membership. Its proceedings were almost universally private and confidential.[6] **A critical study found that of 502 government officials surveyed from 1945 to 1972, more than half were members of the Council.[7]**

Today it has about 5,000 members (including five-year term members[8] between the ages of 30-41), which over its history have included senior serving politicians, more than a dozen Secretaries of State, former national security officers, bankers, lawyers, professors, former CIA members and senior media figures.[citation needed]

In 1962 the group began a program of bringing select Air Force officers to the Harold Pratt House to study alongside its scholars. The Army, Navy and Marine Corps requested they start similar programs for their own officers.[7]

Vietnam created a rift within the organization. When Hamilton Fish Armstrong announced in 1970 that he would be leaving the helm of *Foreign Affairs* after 45 years, new chairman David

Rockefeller approached a family friend, William Bundy, to take over the position. Anti-war advocates within the Council rose in protest against this appointment, *claiming that Bundy's hawkish record in the State and Defense Departments and the CIA precluded him from taking over an independent journal. Some considered Bundy a war criminal for his prior actions.*[7]

Seven American presidents have addressed the Council, two while still in office – Bill Clinton and George W. Bush.[9]

The Council says that it has never sought to serve as a receptacle for government policy papers that cannot be shared with the public and does not encourage its members serving in government to do so. The Council says that discussions at its headquarters remain confidential, not because they share or discuss secret information, but because the system allows members to test new ideas with other members.[10] (Emphasis is mine. Is this an excuse or a reason? Whatever it is, you don't see any of the CFR's policy work in the media.)

Website

It has an extensive website, www.cfr.org, featuring links to its history, fellows' biographical information, think tank, the David Rockefeller Studies Program, Independent Task Force reports[11] and other reports, CFR books, expert interviews, meeting transcripts, audio, and videos, Emmy award-winning multimedia Crisis Guides and timelines, Foreign Affairs, and many other publications, biographies of notable directors and other board members, corporate members, and press releases.[2]

Influence on foreign policy

Beginning in 1939 and lasting for five years, the Council achieved much greater prominence within the government and the State Department when it established the strictly confidential *War and Peace Studies,* funded entirely by the Rockefeller Foundation.[12] The secrecy surrounding this group was such that the Council members who were not involved in its deliberations were completely unaware of the study group's existence.[12]

It was divided into four functional topic groups: economic and financial, security and armaments, territorial, and political. The security and armaments group was headed by Allen Welsh Dulles who later became a pivotal figure in the CIA's predecessor, the OSS. It ultimately produced 682 memoranda for the State Department, marked classified and circulated among the appropriate government departments. As a historical judgment, its overall influence on actual government planning at the time is still said to remain unclear.[12]

In an anonymous piece called "The Sources of Soviet Conduct" that appeared in *Foreign Affairs* in 1947, CFR study group member George Kennan coined the term "containment." The essay would prove to be highly influential in US foreign policy for seven upcoming presidential administrations. 40 years later, Kennan explained that he had never suspected the Russians of any desire to launch an attack on America; he thought that was obvious enough he didn't need to explain it in his essay. William Bundy credited the CFR's study groups with helping to lay the framework of thinking that led to the Marshall Plan and NATO. Due to new interest in the group, membership grew towards 1,000.[13]

Dwight D. Eisenhower chaired a CFR study group while he served as President of Columbia University. One member later said, "whatever General Eisenhower knows about economics, he has learned at the study group meetings."[13] The CFR study group devised an expanded study group called "Americans for Eisenhower" to increase his chances for the presidency. **Eisenhower would later draw many Cabinet members from CFR ranks and become a CFR member himself. His primary CFR appointment was Secretary of State John Foster Dulles**. Dulles gave a public address at the Harold Pratt House in which he announced a new direction for Eisenhower's foreign policy: "There is no local defense which alone will contain the mighty land power of the communist world. Local defenses must be reinforced by the further deterrent of massive retaliatory power." After this speech, the council convened a session on "Nuclear Weapons and Foreign Policy" and chose Henry Kissinger to head it. Kissinger spent the following academic year working on the project at Council headquarters. The book of the same name that he published from his research in 1957 gave him national recognition, topping the national bestseller lists.[13]

On 24 November 1953, a study group heard a report from political scientist William Henderson regarding the ongoing conflict between France and Vietnamese Communist leader Ho Chi Minh's Viet Minh forces, a struggle that would later become known as the First Indochina War. *Henderson argued that Ho's cause was primarily nationalist in nature and that Marxism had "little to do with the current revolution."* **Further, the report said, the United States could work with Ho to guide his movement away from Communism. State Department officials, however, expressed skepticism about direct American intervention in Vietnam and the idea was tabled. Over the next twenty years, the United States would find itself allied with anti-Communist South Vietnam and against Ho and his supporters in the Vietnam War.**[13]

The Council served as a "breeding ground" for important American policies such as mutual deterrence, arms control, and nuclear non-proliferation.[13]

A four-year long study of relations between America and China was conducted by the Council between 1964 and 1968. One study published in 1966 concluded that American citizens were more open to talks with China than their elected leaders. Henry Kissinger had continued to publish in Foreign Affairs and was appointed by President Nixon to serve as National Security Adviser in 1969. In 1971, he embarked on a secret trip to Beijing to broach talks with Chinese leaders. Nixon went to China in 1972, and diplomatic relations were completely normalized by President Carter's Secretary of State, another Council member, Cyrus Vance.[13]

In November 1979, while chairman of the CFR, David Rockefeller became embroiled in an international incident when he and Henry Kissinger, along with John J. McCloy and Rockefeller aides, persuaded President Jimmy Carter through the State Department to admit the Shah of Iran, Mohammad Reza Pahlavi, into the US for hospital treatment for lymphoma. This action directly precipitated what is known as the Iran hostage crisis and placed Rockefeller under intense media scrutiny (particularly from The New York Times) for the first time in his public life.[14][15]

An influential think tank, the Council has been the subject of debates over sovereignty as well as the subject of numerous conspiracy theories. This is primarily due to the number of high-ranking government officials (along with world business leaders and prominent media figures) in its membership and, as documented above, the array of American foreign policy decisions with its members have been involved.[16] In response to the allegations and insinuations, the CFR's website contains a FAQ section about its affairs.[17]

Current policy initiatives

The CFR started a program in 2008 to last for 5 years and funded by a grant from the Robina Foundation called "International Institutions and Global Governance" which aims to identify the institutional requirements for effective multilateral cooperation in the 21st century.[18]

The CFR's Maurice C. Greenberg Center for Geoeconomic Studies, directed by scholar and author Sebastian Mallaby works to promote a better understanding among policymakers, academic specialists, and the interested public of how economic and political forces interact to influence world affairs.[19]

The CFR's Center for Preventive Action (CPA) seeks to help prevent, defuse, or resolve deadly conflicts around the world and to expand the body of knowledge on conflict prevention. It does so by creating a forum in which representatives of governments, international organizations, nongovernmental organizations, corporations, and civil society can gather to develop operational and timely strategies for promoting peace in specific conflict situations.

Membership

Main article: Members of the Council on Foreign Relations

There are two types of membership: life, and term membership, which lasts for 5 years and is available to those between 30 and 36. Only U.S. citizens (native born or naturalized) and permanent residents who have applied for U.S. citizenship are eligible. A candidate for life membership must be nominated in writing by one Council member and seconded by a minimum of three others. Visiting fellows are prohibited from applying for membership until they have completed their fellowship tenure.[20]

Corporate membership (250 in total) is divided into "Basic", "Premium" ($25,000+) and "President's Circle" ($50,000+). All corporate executive members have opportunities to hear distinguished speakers, such as overseas presidents and prime ministers, chairmen and CEOs of multinational corporations, and U.S. officials and Congressmen. President and premium members are also entitled to other benefits, including attendance at small, private dinners or receptions with senior American officials and world leaders.[21]

References

1.^ Lobe, Jim (August 19, 2005). "Realists Rule?". Inter Press Service. "The nation's most influential foreign-policy think tank"

2.^ a b "President's Welcome". Council on Foreign Relations. Retrieved 2007-02-24.

3.^ Wilson, Woodrow. "President Woodrow Wilson's 14 Points (1918)". Our Documents.

4.^ "The Inquiry". History of CFR. Council on Foreign Relations. Retrieved 2007-02-24.

5.^ "Council on Foreign Relations". U.S. Department of Justice. Federal Bureau of Investigation. Retrieved 30 November 2009.

6.^ "Continuing the Inquiry: Basic Assumptions".

7.^ a b c "Consensus Endangered". History of CFR. Council on Foreign Relations. Retrieved 2007-02-24.

8.^ "Term Member Program"

9.^ "American Presidents at the Council on Foreign Relations". Barack Obama spoke at the CFR as a U.S. Senator in 2005 on the issue of nuclear proliferation.

10.^ "The Second Transformation". History of CFR. Council on Foreign Relations. Retrieved 2007-02-24.

11.^ "Independent Task Force reports". Council on Foreign Relations. Retrieved 2009-10-08.

12.^ a b c "Continuing the Inquiry: War and Peace"

13.^ a b c d e f "Continuing the Inquiry: "X" Leads the Way"

14.^ Rothbard, Murray, Why the War? The Kuwait Connection (May 1991)

15.^ Scrutiny by NYT over the Shah of Iran - David Rockefeller, Memoirs (pp.356-75)

16.^ Kay, Jonathan (2011). Among the Truthers: A Journey Through America's Growing Conspiracist Underground. HarperCollins. pp. 1-22. ISBN 0-06-200481-6.

17.^ Frequently Asked Questions about the CFR

18.^ "International Institutions and Global Governance". Council on Foreign Relations. Retrieved 2010-06-01.

19.^ "Maurice C. Greenberg Center for Geoeconomic Studies". Council on Foreign Relations. Retrieved 2010-06-01.

20.^ "Membership".

21.^ "Corporate Program"PDF (330 KiB).

This page was last modified on 30 May 2012.

No discussion of Communism in the United States would be complete without some thoughts from Saul Alinsky's *Rules for Radicals*. The book may not have been on the New York Times best seller list, but it influenced the socialist/communist movement in the U. S. It led to the formation of ACORN (Association of Community Organizations for Reform Now) with some assistance from the world famous community organizer, not yet president, Barack Hussein Obama.

Here are some excerpts and quotations from...

Saul Alinsky's School for Radicals

Alinsky's *Rules for Radicals*: "Known as the 'father of modern American radicalism,' Saul D. Alinsky (1909-1972) developed strategies and tactics that take the enormous, unfocused emotional energy of grassroots groups and transform it into effective antigovernment and anti-corporate activism. ... Some of these rules are ruthless, but they work."

Hillary Clinton's 1969 Political Science Thesis ("There is Only the Fight") refers to an earlier version of Alinsky's training manual. "In 1946," she wrote, "Alinsky's first book, *Reveille for Radicals,* was published."

Note: See also, *From Freedom to Servitude)* (2009) by Berit Kjos; *Training a socialist army of world servers* (2008) by Berit Kjos; *From Marx to Lenin, Gramsci & Alinsky* excerpts from *The Keys of this Blood* (1990) by Malachi Martin; *Real Conspiracies: Past and Present* by Berit Kjos.

Conspiracies—Past & Present

Background information

"Obama learned his lesson well. I am proud to see that my father's model for organizing is being applied successfully beyond local community organizing to affect the Democratic campaign in 2008. It is a fine tribute to Saul Alinsky as we approach his 100th birthday." --Letter from L. DAVID ALINSKY, son of Neo-Marxist Saul Alinsky.

Note: Obama helped fund the 'Alinsky Academy' by way of his directorship at The Woods Fund, a nonprofit on which Obama served as paid director, with William Charles (Bill) Ayers former Weather Underground terrorist, from 1999 to December 2002. The Woods Fund provided startup funding and later capital to the Midwest Academy.... 'Midwest describes itself as 'one of the nation's oldest and best-known schools for community organizations, citizen organizations and individuals committed to progressive social change.'... Midwest teaches Alinsky tactics of community organizing.

Hillary, Obama and the Cult of Alinsky: "True revolutionaries do not flaunt their radicalism," Alinsky taught. "They cut their hair, put on suits and infiltrate the system from within." Alinsky viewed revolution as a slow, patient process. The trick was to penetrate existing institutions such as churches, unions and political parties.... Many leftists view Hillary as a sell-out because she claims to hold moderate views on some issues. However, Hillary is simply following Alinsky's counsel to do and say whatever it takes to gain power.

"Obama is also an Alinskyite.... Obama spent years teaching workshops on the Alinsky method. In 1985 he began a four-year stint as a community organizer in Chicago, working for an Alinskyite group called the Developing Communities Project.... Camouflage is key to Alinsky-style organizing. While trying to build coalitions of black churches in Chicago, Obama caught flak for not attending church himself. He became an instant churchgoer." (By Richard Poe, 11-27-07)

Rules for Radicals
By Saul Alinsky - 1971

Opening page - Dedication

"Lest we forget at least an over-the-shoulder acknowledgment to the very first radical: from all our legends, mythology, and history... the first radical known to man who rebelled against the establishment and did it so effectively that he at least won his own kingdom — Lucifer."

Prologue

"The Revolutionary force today has two targets, moral as well as material. Its young protagonists are one moment reminiscent of the idealistic early Christians, yet they also urge violence and cry, 'Burn the system down!' They have no illusions about the system, but plenty of illusions about the way to change our world. It is to this point that I have written this book."

---

1. The Purpose

In this book we are concerned with how to create mass organizations to seize power and give it to the people; to realize the democratic dream of equality, justice, peace.... "Better to die on your feet than to live on your knees.' This means revolution." pg.3

"Radicals must be resilient, adaptable to shifting political circumstances, and sensitive enough to the process of action and reaction to avoid being trapped by their own tactics and forced to travel a road not of their choosing." pg.6

"A Marxist begins with his prime truth that all evils are caused by the exploitation of the proletariat by the capitalists. From this he logically proceeds to the revolution to end capitalism, then into the third stage of reorganization into a new social order of the dictatorship of the proletariat, and finally the last stage -- the political paradise of communism." pg.10

"An organizer working in and for an open society is in an ideological dilemma to begin with, he does not have a fixed truth -- truth to him is relative and changing; everything to him is relative and changing.... To the extent that he is free from the shackles of dogma, he can respond to the realities of the widely different situations...." pp.10-11

Notes on Saul Alinsky and Neo-Marxism:

Alinsky's tactics were based, not on Stalin's revolutionary violence, but on the Neo-Marxist strategies of Antonio Gramsci, an Italian Communist. Relying on gradualism, infiltration and the dialectic process rather than a bloody revolution, Gramsci's transformational Marxism was so subtle that few even noticed the deliberate changes.

Like Alinsky, Mikhail Gorbachev followed Gramsci, not Lenin. In fact, Gramsci aroused Stalins's wrath by suggesting that Lenin's revolutionary plan wouldn't work in the West. Instead **the primary assault would be on Biblical absolutes and Christian values, which must be crushed as a social force before the new face of Communism could rise and flourish.**

Malachi Martin gave us a progress report:

"By 1985, the influence of traditional Christian philosophy in the West was weak and negligible.... Gramsci's master strategy was now feasible. Humanly speaking, it was no longer too tall an order to strip large majorities of men and women in the West of those last vestiges that remained to them of Christianity's transcendent God."

2. Of Means and Ends [Forget moral or ethical considerations]

"The end is what you want, the means is how you get it. Whenever we think about-social change, the question of means and ends arises. The man of action views the issue of means and ends in pragmatic and strategic terms. He has no other problem; he thinks only of his actual resources and the possibilities of various choices of action. He asks of ends only whether they are achievable and worth the cost; of means, only whether they will work. ... The real arena is corrupt and bloody." pg.24

"The means-and-ends moralists, constantly obsessed with the ethics of the means used by the Have-Nots against the Haves, should search themselves as to their real political position. In fact, they are passive — but real — allies of the Haves.... The most unethical of all means is the non-use of any means... The standards of judgment must be rooted in the whys and wherefores of life as it is lived, the world as it is, not our wished-for fantasy of the world as it should be..." pps.25-26

"The third rule of ethics of means and ends is that in war the end justifies almost-any means..." pg.29

"The seventh rule... is that generally success or failure is a mighty determinant of ethics pg.34

"The tenth rule is you do what you can with what you have and clothe it with moral garments.... It involves sifting the multiple factors which combine in creating the circumstances at any given time... Who, and how many will support-the action?... If weapons are needed, then are appropriate weapons available? Availability of means determines whether you will be underground or above ground; whether you will move quickly or slowly..." pg.36

Notes: Apparently, Michelle Obama referred to these words during her Democratic National Convention speech:

"She said, 'Barack stood up that day,' talking about a visit to Chicago neighborhoods, 'and spoke words that have stayed with me ever since. He talked about 'The world as it is' and 'The world as it should be...' And, 'All of us driven by a simple belief that the world as it is just won't do – that we have an obligation to, fight for the world as it should be."

Do you wonder who -- or whose values -- should determine what "the world... should be?"

4. The Education of the Organizer

"To the organizer, imagination is the dynamism that starts and sustains him in his whole life of action as an organizer. It ignites and feeds the force that drives him to organize for change..."

"The organizer knows that the real action is in the reaction of the opposition. To   realistically appraise and anticipate the probable reactions of the enemy, he must be able to identify with them, too, in his imagination, and foresee their reactions to his actions...

"The organizers searching with a free and open mind void of certainty, hating dogma, finds laughter not just a way to maintain his sanity but also a key to understanding life." pps.74-75

"...the organizer must be able to split himself into two parts -- one part in the arena of action where he polarizes the issue to 100 to nothing, and helps to lead his forces into conflict, while the other part knows that when the time comes for negotiations that it really is only a 10 percent difference." pg.78

"...the organizer is constantly creating new out of the old. He knows that all new ideas arise from conflict; [See Dialectic Process] that every time man as had a new idea it has been a challenge to the sacred ideas of the past and the present and inevitably a conflict has raged." pg.79

5. Communication [Notice the emphasis on conflict, dialogue, relationships, etc. Team "service" is essential to building strong relationships through "common involvements"]

-"And so the guided questioning goes on without anyone losing face or being left out of the decision-making. Every weakness of every proposed tactic is probed by questions.... Is this manipulation? Certainly..." pg.88

"One of the factors that changes what you can and can't communicate is relationships. There are sensitive areas that one does not touch until there is a strong personal relationship based on common involvements. Otherwise the other party turns off and literally does not hear..."

"Conversely, if you have a good relationship, he is very receptive.... For example, I have always believed that birth control and abortion are personal rights to be exercised by the individual. If, in my early days when I organized... neighborhood in Chicago, which was 95 per cent Roman Catholic, I had tried to communicate this, even through the experience of the residents, whose economic plight was aggravated by large families, that would have been the end of my relationship with the community. That instant I would have been stamped as an enemy of the church and all communication would have ceased.

"Some years later, after establishing solid relationships, I was free to talk about anything.... By then the argument was no longer limited to such questions as, 'How much longer do you think the Catholic Church can hang on to this archaic notion and still survive?' ...the subject and nature of the discussion would have been unthinkable without that solid relationship." pps.93-94

6. In the Beginning: The Process of Power [Notice the compromise needed to build the power base. Yet, since pragmatism has eroded all values, it's simply a matter of ends justifying means. It's not unlike churches that attract members through the world's

111

entertainment -- then continue to soften or hide Truth in order to keep them happy and lure more.]

"From the moment the organizer enters a community he lives, dreams... only one thing and that is to build the mass power base of what he calls the army. Until he has developed that mass power base, he confronts no major issues.... Until he has those means and power instruments, his 'tactics' are very different from power tactics. Therefore, every move revolves around one central point: how many recruits will this bring into the organization, whether by means of local organizations, churches, service groups, labor Unions, corner gangs, or as individuals."

"Change comes from power, and power comes from organization." pg.113

"The first step in community organization is community disorganization. The disruption of the present organization is the first step toward community organization. Present arrangements must be disorganized if they are to be displace by new patterns.... All change means disorganization of the old and organization of the new." pg.116

Compare with this excerpt from "Group Decision and Social Change" by Kurt Lewin:

"A change toward a higher level of group performance is frequently short lived: after a "shot in the arm", group life soon returns to the previous level. This indicates that it does not suffice to define the objective of a planned change in group performance as the reaching of a different level. Permanency of the new level, or permanency for a desired period, should be included in the objective. A successful change includes therefore three aspects:

UNFREEZING (if necessary) the present level...
MOVING to the new level . . . and

FREEZING group life on the new level."

"An organizer must stir up dissatisfaction and discontent... He must create a mechanism that can drain off the underlying guilt for having

112

accepted the previous situation for so long a time. Out of this mechanism, a new community organization arises..."

"The job then is getting the people to move, to act, to participate; in short, to develop and harness the necessary power to effectively conflict with the prevailing patterns and change them. When those prominent in the status quo turn and label you an 'agitator' they are completely correct, for that is, in one word, your function—to agitate to the point of conflict." pg.117

"Process tells us how. Purpose tells us why. But in reality, it is academic to draw a line between them, they are part of a continuum.... Process is really purpose." pg.122

—from Chapter 7.

Tactics

"Tactics are those conscious deliberate acts by which human beings live with each other and deal with the world around them. ... Here our concern is with the tactic of taking; how the Have-Nots can take power away from the Haves." pg.126

Always remember the first rule of power tactics (pps.127-134):

1. "Power is not only what you have, but what the enemy thinks you have."

2. "Never go outside the expertise of your people. When an action or tactic is outside the experience of the people, the result is confusion, fear and retreat...- [and] the collapse of communication.

3. "Whenever possible, go outside the expertise of the enemy. Look for ways to increase insecurity, anxiety and uncertainty. (This happens all the time. Watch how many organizations under attack are blind-sided by seemingly irrelevant arguments that they are then forced to address.)

4. "Make the enemy live up to its own book of rules. You can kill them with this, for they can no more obey their own rules than the Christian church can live up to Christianity."

5. "Ridicule is man's most potent weapon. It is almost impossible to counteract ridicule. Also it infuriates the opposition, which then reacts to your advantage."

6. "A good tactic is one your people enjoy."

7. "A tactic that drags on too long becomes a drag. Man can sustain militant interest in any issue for only a limited time...."

8. "Keep the pressure on, with different tactics and actions, and utilize all events of the period for your purpose."

9. "The threat is usually more terrifying than the thing itself."

10. "The major premise for tactics is the development of operations that will maintain a constant pressure upon the opposition. It is this unceasing pressure that results in the reactions from the opposition that are essential for the success of the campaign."

11. "If you push a negative hard and deep enough, it will break through into its counterside... every positive has its negative."

12. "The price of a successful attack is a constructive alternative."

13. Pick the target, freeze it, personalize it, and polarize it. In conflict tactics there are certain rules that [should be regarded] as universalities. One is that the opposition must be singled out as the target and 'frozen.'

"...any target can always say, 'Why do you center on me when there are others to blame as-well?' When your 'freeze the target,' you disregard these [rational but distracting] arguments....-Then, as you zero in and freeze your target and carry out your attack, all the 'others' come out of the woodwork very soon. They become visible by their support of the target...'

"One acts decisively only in the conviction that all the angels are on one side and all the devils on the other." (pps.127-134)

Notes from an article by Phyllis Schalfly titled "Alinski's Rules: Must Reading In Obama Era," posted at www.ibdeditorials.com/IBDArticles.aspx?id=318470857908277 (2-2-09)

"Alinsky's second chapter, called Of Means and Ends, craftily poses many difficult moral dilemmas, and his 'Tenth Rule of the Ethics of Means and Ends' is: 'you do what you can with what you have and clothe it with moral arguments.' He doesn't ignore traditional moral standards or dismiss them as unnecessary. He is much more devious; he teaches his followers that 'Moral rationalization is indispensable at all times of action whether to justify the selection or the use of ends or means.'"

"The qualities Alinsky looked for in a good organizer were:

ego ("reaching for the highest level for which man can reach — to create, to be a 'great creator,' to play God"),

curiosity (raising "questions that agitate, that break through the accepted pattern"),

irreverence ("nothing is sacred"; the organizer "detests dogma, defies any finite definition of morality"),

imagination ("the fuel for the force that keeps an organizer organizing"),

a sense of humor ("the most potent weapons known to mankind are satire and ridicule"),

an organized personality with confidence in presenting the right reason for his actions only "as a moral rationalization after the right end has been achieved.'

115

"'The organizer's first job is to create the issues or problems,' and 'organizations must be based on many issues.' The organizer 'must first rub raw the resentments of the people of the community; fan the latent hostilities of many of the people to the point of overt expression. He must search out controversy and issues, rather than avoid them, for unless there is controversy people are not concerned enough to act. An organizer must stir up dissatisfaction and discontent.'"

Final thoughts...

If you've had the mental discipline to stay with this collection of fairly recent historical events, biographies, and ideologies, you will begin to piece together the reason for our current econo-political predicament. And this is only the portion that touches on the subversive political side of the ledger.

When you dig into the economic situation, you'll find even more information which will frustrate you. The progressive liberal sector of the political establishment lives and dies by Keynesian economics which is the foundation for the socio-economic policies of those who inhabit the White House, the Treasury, the Federal Reserve Bank, and academia. But, that's another story for another time.

Then, you can tackle the subject of academics in the U. S. and how it's had such a subversive effect since about 1930 when John Dewey became our guru of education. That, too, is another story for another time.

Generally speaking, it looks as if we may have an oligarchy rather than a republican democracy, even though the representatives are chosen by the electoral process as prescribed by the Constitution. The general election of 2012 will be the deciding factor for the future of the nation.

Just for fun, let's take a look at the opening paragraphs of the *Declaration of Independence* and the *Preamble* to the *Constitution* to see if the character of government today still agrees with the objectives of our Founding Fathers.

When in the Course of human events, it becomes necessary for one people to dissolve the political bands which have connected them with another, and to assume among the powers of the earth, the separate and equal station to which the Laws of Nature and of Nature's God entitle them, a decent respect to the opinions of mankind requires that they should declare the causes which impel them to the separation.

We hold these truths to be self-evident, that all men are created equal, that they are endowed by their Creator with certain unalienable Rights, that among these are Life, Liberty and the pursuit of Happiness. — That to secure these rights, Governments are instituted among Men, deriving their just powers from the consent of the governed, — That whenever any Form of Government becomes destructive of these ends, it is the Right of the People to alter or to abolish it, and to institute new Government, laying its foundation on such principles and organizing its powers in such form, as to them shall seem most likely to effect their Safety and Happiness. Prudence, indeed, will dictate that Governments long established should not be changed for light and transient causes; and accordingly all experience hath shewn, that mankind are more disposed to suffer, while evils are sufferable, than to right themselves by abolishing the forms to which they are accustomed. But when a long train of abuses and usurpations, pursuing invariably the same Object evinces a design to reduce them under absolute Despotism, it is their right, it is their duty, to throw off such Government, and to provide new Guards for their future security.

Now, the *Preamble to the Constitution...*

We the People of the United States, in Order to form a more perfect Union, establish Justice, insure domestic Tranquility, provide for the common defence, promote the general Welfare, and secure the Blessings of Liberty to ourselves and our Posterity, do ordain and establish this Constitution for the United States of America.

It's hard to argue with the wisdom of those words, but there are those who would have us believe they're obsolete. Our academic elite and many politicians are leading the charge on the concept of obsolescence which prevails in our education system and in the minds of many of our legislators today.

So...what do you do now? You've taken a step, albeit a small one, in becoming informed. The next is up to you. A Tea Party chapter in your town, city, or suburb will be very beneficial in enabling you to stay informed about the political climate at the local, state, and national level. They do the job the media won't do for you any longer. You're going to have to decide for yourself if you want to join the grassroots millions who have become active because they had to, not because they wanted to. No one else can do it for you. The choice is yours—freedom and liberty or the oppression and misery of socialism.

Sleep well...

Appendix

In order to give you a little better insight into the Communist movement and the union movement and the power they have in the United States, I've taken material directly from various websites to make my point. Their objectives are fairly obvious.

Wikipedia is also frequently used for data. There are a few editorial comments and highlights made by moi for emphasis.

Communist Party USA and labor unions

WHY JOIN?

Members of the Communist Party USA are dedicated to helping advance the day-to-day struggles of the working class and all people on the road to a socialist USA.

We believe that our radical ideas must be paired with real politics. Winning working people's struggles today is the only way to achieve socialism in the future. The heart of our organization is our strategic policy. Our strategy is outlined in our program, The Road to Socialism USA.

Our organization is made up of grassroots community, labor and student activists, national movement leaders, young and old, immigrant and native-born. We are electricians, writers, steelworkers, teachers, retail workers, students, small business people and more. We are working, unemployed and active retirees. We are women and men. Our members are African American, white, Latino, Asian, Pacific Islander, Arab, American Indian and from every nationality. They speak English, Spanish, Portuguese, Chinese and dozens more languages. We are gay and straight. We come from every region and state of this country, from big cities to small towns, from coast to coast.

World communist parties: "Socialism is the future"

by: Susan Webb
January 3, 2012
tags: Socialism, communism, global economy, CPUSA, internationalism

ATHENS - "Socialism is the future" was the theme of a meeting here of communist and workers parties from 59 countries last month. The question, of course, was how to get to socialism. Varied views were expressed on this. (Note to Glenn Beck types who conjure up a monolithic "world communist conspiracy": it just ain't so.)

At the same time, the meeting demonstrated that those who say socialism is dead need to think again.

An array of countries were represented where communist and workers parties lead or are part of the government. These include not only countries like Cuba, Vietnam and Laos, but also, for example, Guyana, where the People's Progressive Party has led the government for 19 years; South Africa, where communists, as members of the African National Congress, serve in government; Cyprus, whose president is a leader of the Progressive Party of Working People (AKEL); and a number of Latin American countries such as Brazil and Paraguay, where communists hold positions in governments led by allied progressive forces.

The gathering, hosted by the Communist Party of Greece, was held Dec. 9-11 at the height of the economic crisis there.

Pointing to "the deep and prolonged capitalist crisis" prevailing internationally, including in the U.S., the meeting's final statement noted, "It becomes increasingly obvious for millions of working people that the crisis is a crisis of the system."

Many speakers referred to the Occupy Wall Street movement as an indication of this emerging sentiment. The Communist Party USA delegate spoke of a "surge in united action by labor and major organizations of the African American and Latino people and other democratic forces."

The Portuguese Communist Party representative said, "The attempt to make working people pay for the crisis is spurring the organized working-class

120

struggle in several countries ... and leading to hugely diverse demonstrations that reveal capitalism's shrinking support base, and the availability of other anti-monopoly strata to struggle."

He continued, "There is a potential to build broad social alliances that ... can contribute toward a needed struggle against the dominant big-business policies and toward building democratic, patriotic and anti-monopoly alternatives."

The South African delegate emphasized that the whole of the left "needs to take up in earnest [the] ecological destruction caused by the rampant accumulation of capitalism." The meeting adopted the South African Communist Party's proposal for an international conference of communist and workers parties specifically on climate justice, to be held in 2012 in South Africa.

Discussion was also shaped by the "Arab Spring" uprisings and continuing popular struggles in North Africa and the Middle East.

The Turkish Communist Party's delegate warned that today's imperialist policymakers see "political Islam" - groups like the Muslim Brotherhood or Turkey's ruling Islamist party - as "compatible" with imperialism.

"The Muslim Brothers are ready to serve the imperialists," the Jordanian Communist Party representative said. U.S. policy, she said, "is based on creating an alliance with the Islamists and even the fundamentalists." The Lebanese representative declared that "Turkey is spearheading the imperialist efforts in the Arab world and the Middle East."

Likewise, several Middle Eastern parties warned that the feudal Gulf states are acting as agents of the U.S. and other capitalist powers, funneling cash, arms and other forms of assistance to "strengthen the conservatives and the Islamists," as the Jordanian representative put it.

As to how to deal with the current crisis and how to get to socialism, parties projected differing approaches.

The leader of the Communist Party of Greece said no proposal to deal with the crisis can "constitute a pro-people way out ... unless it poses as a question of principle the rupture ... with capitalist ownership, its state institutions, its international alliances."

She spoke of "the regroupment of the workers' and people's movement with a clear anti-imperialist antimonopoly orientation, anti-capitalist in the final analysis." A policy of alliances, she said, can go only two ways: either aim at the prolongation of bourgeois political power, or aim for the overthrow of the bourgeois government.

On the other hand, the representative of the Communist Party of Brazil (PCdoB) spoke of the participation of communist parties in Latin America and the Caribbean in different kinds of broad progressive political fronts that govern their countries. These fronts, he said, "are part of a tactical process of accumulation of forces, within the borders of capitalism." This, he said, advances the strategic objective of winning political power in order to start the transition to socialism.

He, and a number of others, emphasized that "there is not a single and non-historical model of revolutionary process neither of construction of socialism."

"What we have is a set of principles, formulated by Marx and Lenin and developed by other revolutionaries. Socialism is universal as a general theory and desire for freedom of the working class and the peoples in the entire world. But socialism takes on national features ... it is accomplished according to the social formation and the particular historical conditions of each people."

That, he said, requires from communists, "in each country, the elaboration of original programs and the formulation of strategies and tactics that are adequate to present times."

Highlights from CPUSA's 29th Convention, includes video

by: Rick Nagin
May 26 2010
tags: video, Communist Party USA, ultra-right, socialism, elections

Note from the author: The following is an e-mail sent by *People's World* writer Rick Nagin to hundreds of his friends, family members, and acquaintances in Ohio.

Brothers and Sisters -

I had the great pleasure of attending the 29th National Convention of the Communist Party USA this past weekend in New York. It was a very inspiring event and I want to share some highlights.

The convention reaffirmed the party's basic position of working with labor and its allies to build a broad democratic coalition to defeat the ultra-right. The party sees this as necessary to defend the rights of working people at present as well as key in the long run to weaken corporate power and move towards working class power (socialism).

The immediate challenge is to defend and, if possible, extend the gains made in 2006 and 2008 by setting back the right-wing attempt to regain power in the November midterm elections.

In addition, the convention called for helping to build mass fight back against the economic crisis, especially on the issue of jobs as well as defending the gains won in the health care reform. There was an excellent PowerPoint presentation on the economic crisis and what needs to be done to overcome it.

Defeating the right-wing's use of racism and anti-immigrant hysteria was seen as critical to success in both the electoral and economic arenas.

Workshops and plenary panels on were held on the elections, labor, African American equality, Latino equality, peace, youth, the environment, public education, women's rights, gay rights, and work in the religious community and growing the party and Young Communist League. Detailed resolutions on six broad areas were adopted.

Like all conventions there was a lot of hoop-la and fanfare. Each session opened with a cultural presentation and there was a lot of singing. There was also an evening celebration and cultural event on the Party's 90th anniversary with great live music and dancing.

The Democratic State Assemblyman representing the district where the convention was held gave a great speech welcoming the convention as did several local union presidents. We also heard from Communists holding local office in a number of states.

Leadership was elected including Sam Webb as national chairman, Jarvis Tyner as vice chairman and Roberta Wood as secretary-treasurer.

The convention was united and enthusiastic and delegates left with renewed confidence and determination to work to consolidate the defeat of the ultra-right and move forward to repair the damage they have caused to democracy and the rights of working people.

The main reports, resolutions the PowerPoint presentation will soon be available at the cpusa.org website where there is also a video of the opening session. Reports on the convention are on the peoplesworld.org website. Ohio delegates are anxious to meet with groups to discuss the convention and how to move ahead. Let me know if you would like to set up a meeting.

AFL-CIO

Our Mission and Vision

The AFL-CIO exists to represent people who work. The mission of the AFL-CIO is expressed in our Constitution:

The American Federation of Labor and Congress of Industrial Organizations is an expression of the hopes and aspirations of the working people of America.

We resolve to fulfill the yearning of the human spirit for liberty, justice and community; to advance individual and associational freedom; to vanquish - oppression, privation and cruelty in all their forms; and to join with all persons, of whatever nationality or faith, who cherish the cause of democracy and the call of solidarity, to grace the planet with these achievements.

We dedicate ourselves to improving the lives of working families, bringing fairness and dignity to the workplace and securing social equity in the Nation.

The AFL-CIO envisions a future in which work and all people who work are valued, respected and rewarded. While the AFL-CIO represents millions of working people who belong to unions and have the benefits of union membership, the labor federation embraces all people who share the common bond of work.

Work is what we do to better ourselves, to build dreams and to support our families. But work is more than that. Work cures, creates, builds, innovates and shapes the future. Work connects us all.

The AFL-CIO is an organization of people who work. *We help lead a movement for social and economic justice in America and the world.* Author's note: They might as well say..."Workers of the world—unite!"— the familiar words of Karl Marx in his *Communist Manifesto.*

The current president of the AFL-CIO is Richard Trumka. Just for grins, here are a couple of his fairly recent statements:

> "The reality is that they are an ideologically, politically-motivated and anti-union front group." Talking about the Associated General Contractors. May, 2012 *National Journal*

> "The Republican party has said, from Mitt Romney on down, they are against workers," he said "It's not about fairness, it's not about enforcing the law, it's about making [labor] weaker."- May 6, 2012 *National Journal*

Author's note: When they use the phrase "people who work" what does that bring to mind? Most people work for a living one way or another. Are they postulating that only the hourly paid employee is the one who works? This is pure Marxist rubbish.

SEIU
Service Employees International Union

We are the Service Employees International Union, an organization of 2.1 million members united by the belief in the dignity and worth of workers and the services they provide and dedicated to improving the lives of workers and their families and *creating a more just and humane society.* (Emphasis is mine.)

- SEIU Mission Statement

Copied from the website on June 20, 2012.PART A: PREAMBLE AND APPLICABILITY

SEIU believes in the dignity and worth of all workers. We have dedicated ourselves to improving the lives of workers and their families and to *creating a more just and humane society.* We are *committed to pursuing justice for all, and in particular to bringing economic and social justice to those most exploited in our community.* In order to achieve our mission, we must develop highly trained and motivated leaders at every level of the Union who reflect the membership in all of its diversity. (Note from author: When you see references to social justice and exploitation, you know you're dealing with a radical socialist organization.)

A Closer Look Inside Labor's Fastest-Growing Union

Website 6-20-12

The 2.1 million-member Service Employees International Union is the fastest-growing union in North America, and its membership is among the most diverse in the labor movement. Since 1996, 1.2 million workers in three key sectors have united with SEIU, making it the largest healthcare union, with members in hospitals, nursing homes, and home care; the largest property services union with members in the building cleaning and security industries, including janitors, security officers, superintendents, maintenance workers, window cleaners, and doormen and women; and the second largest public employee union with more than 1 million local and state government workers, public school employees, bus drivers, and child care providers.

» SEIU is taking bold actions to unite the nine out of 10 non-union workers in America. We continue to work with our partners in the labor, progressive and religious communities to launch innovative campaigns that bring new

126

hope and opportunity to workers in today's global economy. SEIU helped form Change to Win, a labor federation representing nearly six million members with the Teamsters, the United Food and Commercial Workers, along with the Laborers and the United Farm Workers, to develop strategic, industry-based organizing campaigns to unite workers' strength. We will continue working with our members and partners to challenge the CEOs and politicians that contributed to our nation's economic collapse and to help put the country back on the path of economic growth for all working families.

» SEIU is building a 21st-century global union to help ensure that workers, not just corporations and CEOs, benefit from today's global economy. SEIU is working with unions in similar industries across the globe to challenge multi-nationals to provide comparable wages and benefits, and allow workers in every country the freedom to form unions. SEIU members have joined workers from France and Great Britain and members of Unison and the CGT and French labor federation CFDT, in global delegations on both sides of the Atlantic. And, unionists from around the world have come together with SEIU to hold civil disobedience rallies, march with workers and met one-on-one with workers in a commitment to take the stories of U.S. workers to the management of international companies based and operating overseas.

» SEIU is committed to giving healthcare workers a voice on the job and providing the best care for the people they serve. As the largest healthcare union in the country, we were a major player in winning historic healthcare reform legislation with a comprehensive approach to expanding coverage, controlling costs, and improving quality for all Americans. Most recently:

•16,000 SEIU Healthcare Florida workers overwhelmingly voted to join 1199SEIU United Healthcare Workers East;

•12,000 Missouri home care attendants in the Consumer Directed Services program have united in the Missouri Home Care Union (which includes SEIU); and

•5,500 Wisconsin home care workers voted overwhelmingly 'yes' to united with SEIU in one of the state's largest union elections in decades.

In addition to organizing healthcare workers, SEIU is now driving efforts to provide workers and communities with a clearer understanding of how healthcare reform will impact the lives of SEIU members and all working families through the online resource, Healthcare Reform Starts Now!

» SEIU is helping ensure immigrant workers have a shot at the American dream. Representing more immigrants than any other union, SEIU has been a leading voice for immigration reform that rewards work and improves conditions for all working people in this country. SEIU helped pave the way for organized labor to support legalization for hard-working, tax-paying immigrants, and the union's civic participation program encourages immigrants to actively participate in our communities and our democracy.

» SEIU is transforming the U.S. private security industry by partnering with unions overseas and community allies determined to hold companies accountable on safety and training standards. Employers such as Sweden-based Securitas have now agreed to respect U.S. security officers' freedom to form a union and signaled their willingness to work with SEIU to create good jobs with training. Security officers are also partnering with civil rights organizations, community groups and churches to fight for better wages, affordable health care, and opportunity for career growth for a largely African-American workforce. SEIU is the largest union of security officers in the country, representing over 50,000 officers who work in the public and private sector.

» SEIU is setting a new standard for quality child care services nationwide. Family child care providers in SEIU Illinois, Washington, Oregon, and Maryland have united to win a voice for their profession and the children in their care. They've won training incentives, better access to health care, and pay increases--raising the bar for quality child care services across the country. Now, child care center workers are joining the movement to stabilize the child care workforce by making child care a secure profession, improving funding for child care and early education, and expanding parents' access to affordable, quality care. SEIU is the largest union of child care workers in America, representing more 80,000 early learning and care professionals at Head Start centers, child care centers, and family child care.

» SEIU is the second largest union of public service employees. SEIU members are fighting for fair and stable funding to ensure that Americans have the quality, reliable public services they need. While many states across the country are making drastic cuts to schools and human services that would deepen the recession, SEIU members helped raise $11.8 billion for public services in 15 states this year.

•Members in Oregon helped lead a victorious tax fairness campaign that preserves funding for schools, healthcare, and other public services important to middle class families.

•In California and other states, workers have led campaigns to protect a fair and secure retirement system, and waged successful local ballot initiatives, such as those maintaining emergency Mary Kay Henry was elected President of SEIU by the international union's Executive Board on May 8, 2010, to serve the two remaining years of Stern's term. Her term as President will expire in 2012.[2] After her election, Henry said her major priorities as union president would be to advocate for labor rights, immigrants' rights, and LGBT rights.[4] However, she said she did not foresee bringing SEIU back into the AFL-CIO and refused to end the union's battles with its breakaway California locals.[4] A few days after her election, Henry began conducting a review of the duties and assignments of SEIU's top leadership and staff (including Secretary-Treasurer Burger), noting, "It is the prerogative of the president to reassign responsibilities."[33][34] Burger denied that she was thinking of quitting the union due to the review.[34]medical centers in Los Angeles and Alameda Counties.

SEIU is utilizing an innovative, industry-based model to help lift janitors out of poverty and help companies remain competitive. When over 5,000 janitors in Houston formed a union in late 2005 to cap one of the largest successful organizing drives by private sector workers ever in the U.S. South, they united their strength with SEIU janitors in nearly 30 other major cities who work for the same national cleaning contractors - often in buildings owned by the same large, national real estate companies. The Houston janitors will soon begin negotiating improvement in a single, "master" agreement; in other cities, this has allowed janitors to win health care and pay increases and has ended a "race to the bottom" in which companies vie for contracts by paying janitors as little as possible - instead of competing on issues of quality, efficiency, and innovation.

Author's note:The current president of the SEIU is Mary Kay Henry. I could find no quotations which could be attributed to her, therefore, I include the following from *Wikipedia*:

Mary Kay Henry was elected President of SEIU by the international union's Executive Board on May 8, 2010, to serve the two remaining years of Stern's term. Her term as President will expire in 2012.[2] After her election, Henry said her **major priorities as union president would be to advocate for labor rights, immigrants' rights, and LGBT rights.**[4] However, she said she did not foresee bringing SEIU back into the AFL-CIO and refused to end the union's battles with its breakaway California locals.[4]

National Education Association

 The National Education Association, in contrast to the American Federation of Teachers, was formed as a professional association in 1857 and adopted union activities beginning in the 1960s.
NEA's Vision, Mission, and Values

Adopted at the 2006 NEA Representative Assembly:

The National Education Association

 We, the members of the National Education Association of the United States, are the voice of education professionals. Our work is fundamental to the nation, and we accept the profound trust placed in us.

Our Vision
Our vision is a great public school for every student.

Our Mission
 Our mission is to advocate for education professionals and to unite our members and the nation to fulfill the promise of public education to prepare every student to succeed in a diverse and interdependent world.

Our Core Values
These principles guide our work and define our mission:

Equal Opportunity. We believe public education is the gateway to opportunity. All students have the **human and civil right** to a quality public education that develops their potential, independence, and character.

A Just Society. We believe public education is vital to building respect for the worth, dignity, and equality of every individual in our diverse society.

Democracy. We believe public education is the cornerstone of our republic. Public education provides individuals with the skills to be involved, informed, and engaged in our representative democracy.

Professionalism. We believe that the expertise and judgment of education professionals are critical to student success. We maintain the highest professional standards, and we expect the status, compensation, and respect due all professionals.

Partnership. We believe partnerships with parents, families, communities, and other stakeholders are essential to quality public education and student success.

Collective Action. We believe individuals are strengthened when they work together for the common good. As education professionals, we improve both our professional status and quality of public education when we unite and **advocate collectively**.

NEA also believes every student in America, regardless of family income or place of residence, deserves a quality education. In pursuing its mission, NEA has determined that we will focus the energy and resources of our 3.2 million members on improving the quality of teaching, increasing student achievement and making schools safer, better places to learn.

The words of Dennis Van Roekel, President of the NEA in a publication dated 2-22-12 in The Blog.

> For as long as we have had **struggling** schools in America's cities, there have been efforts to turn them around. Those of us **committed to equal opportunity** have always believed that education gives students a foothold on the ladder to success. Yet recent studies show the role of education as a force for equality is threatened.

Author's note: As you read the above, you see several progressive (communist) buzz words..."equal opportunity", "human and civil right", "advocate collectively". Emphasis is mine.

Political activities (from Wikipedia 6-22-12)

The National Education Association headquarters located at 1201 16th Street, N.W., in downtown Washington, D.C.

NEA has played a role in politics since its founding, as it has sought to influence state and federal laws that would have an impact on public education. Every political position adopted by NEA was brought by one of its members to the annual Representative Assembly, where it was considered on the floor, debated, and voted on by elected delegates.

The organization tracks legislation related to education and the teaching profession and encourages members to get involved in politics through a comprehensive Legislative Action Center on its website.

1912: NEA endorses Women's Suffrage

1919: NEA members in New Jersey lead the way to the nation's first state pension; by 1945, every state had a pension plan in effect

1941: NEA successfully lobbied Congress for special funding for public schools near military bases

1945: NEA lobbied for the G.I. Bill of Rights to help returning soldiers continue their education

1958: NEA helps gain passage of the National Defense Education Act

1964: NEA lobbies to pass the Civil Rights Act

1968: NEA leads an effort to establish the Bilingual Education Act

1974: NEA backs a case heard before the U.S. Supreme Court that proposes to make unlawful the firing of pregnant teachers or forced maternity leave

1984: NEA fights for and wins passage of a federal retirement equity law that provides the means to end sex discrimination against women in retirement funds

2000s: NEA has lobbied for changes to the No Child Left Behind Act

2009: NEA delegates to the Representative Assembly pass a resolution that opposes the discriminatory treatment of same-sex couples.[41]

In recent decades the NEA has increased its visibility in party politics, endorsing more Democratic Party candidates and contributing funds and other assistance to political campaigns. The NEA asserts itself as "non-partisan", but critics point out that the NEA has endorsed and provided support for every Democratic Party presidential nominee from Jimmy Carter to Barack Obama and has never endorsed any Republican or third party candidate for the presidency.[42][43] However, NEA has endorsed and supported Republican political candidates for Congressional and

Gubernatorial offices. In 2006, NEA funded over 300 candidates, a list which included Democrats, Republicans and Independents, such as Mike Simpson, Richard Lugar, Olympia Snowe, Jim Gerlach, John M. McHugh and Bernard Sanders, among others.

Based on required filings with the federal government, it is estimated that between 1990 and 2002 eighty percent of the NEA's substantial political contributions went to Democratic Party candidates.[citation needed] Although this has been questioned as being out of balance with the more diverse political views of the broader membership,[44] the NEA maintains that it bases support for candidates primarily on the organization's interpretation of candidates' support for public education and educators. Every Presidential candidate endorsed by NEA must be approved by majority vote among the members themselves at NEA's annual Representative Assembly.

Others benefitting from NEA funding, according to the most recent filings, include Jesse Jackson's Rainbow/PUSH Coalition, Center for American Progress, Media Matters for America, National Council of La Raza, the Gay and Lesbian Alliance Against Defamation, Amnesty International, the now-defunct ACORN,[45] and AIDS Walk Washington.[8]

The NEA is a leading member of the U.S. Global Leadership Coalition, a Washington D.C.-based coalition of over 400 major companies and NGOs that advocates for a larger International Affairs Budget, which funds American diplomatic and development efforts abroad.[46]

Author's note: This is alarming inasmuch it plays into the Agenda 21 programs.

American Federation of Teachers, AFL-CIO

Author's note: Most of the ensuing data comes from *Wikipedia*. The material regarding political activity comes from the latest postings to *Wikipedia* as of June 22, 2012. You'll find the political activities very interesting.

The AFT was founded on April 15, 1916 as a labor union. (The National Education Association, by contrast, formed as a professional association in

1857 and adopted union activities beginning in the 1960s). Currently, the union has a membership of about 1.1 million give or take a few thousand.

Five divisions within the AFT represent the broad spectrum of the AFT's membership: pre-K through 12th-grade teachers; paraprofessionals and other school-related personnel; higher education faculty and professional staff; federal, state and local government employees; and nurses and other healthcare professionals. In addition, the AFT represents approximately 80,000 early childhood educators and nearly 250,000 retiree members.

The AFT is governed by its elected officers and by delegates to the union's biennial convention, which sets union policy. Elected leaders are Randi Weingarten, president; Lorretta Johnson, secretary-treasurer; Francine Lawrence, executive vice president; and a 43-member executive council.

Political and civil rights activities

In 1963, the AFT (unlike many other unions) actively supported the March on Washington for Jobs and Freedom organized by civil rights leaders, at which Dr. Martin Luther King, Jr. delivered his "I Have a Dream" speech. Busloads of AFT members came to the nation's capital for the event.

In 1964, Albert Shanker was elected president of the UFT (United Federation of Teachers. This union represents the New York City school teachers.)

In 1965, the UFT put its funds in a bank that refused to have dealings with the apartheid regime in South Africa—20 years before most other unions began to campaign against apartheid.

In 1967, the New York State Legislature passed the Taylor Law, which provided collective bargaining rights to public employees (but prohibiting them to strike). The AFT began rapidly organizing new members in New York state. Nearby states such as Rhode Island, Connecticut, Pennsylvania and New Jersey also saw large membership increases.

The same year, the UFT held a three-week strike for smaller class sizes. Shanker was jailed in the Sing-Sing state prison for 15 days for violating the Taylor Law's prohibition on public employee strikes.

In 1967, under AFT president Charlie Cogen, the union's headquarters was moved to Washington, D.C., occupying several buildings on and around Dupont Circle, growing out of its office space several times. In 1985, the AFT built its current headquarters at 555 New Jersey Avenue N.W.

Ocean Hill-Brownsville strike

On May 8, 1968 the union held a one-day strike in the Ocean Hill-Brownsville school district. The city of New York established the Ocean Hill-Brownsville area of Brooklyn as one of three decentralized school districts in 1968 in an effort to give the minority community more say in school affairs. The school district operated under a separate, community-elected governing board with the power to hire administrators.

The experiment had the early support of the UFT. But the UFT also argued that the new school district should retain its most experienced teachers in the schools.

The crisis began when the governing board fired 13 teachers and six administrators for what the board said were efforts to sabotage the decentralization experiment. Under the terms of the decentralization agreement, the teachers were returned to the control of the New York City public school system, where they sat idle in the school district offices.

UFT president Albert Shanker demanded due process. He declared that the UFT would not be passive while teachers were removed without specific charges being filed and without a chance to defend themselves.

Many observers argued that the decentralization experiment was a canard. Little educational advancement for the poverty-stricken students of Ocean Hill-Brownsville could be achieved without additional resources, which were not provided. But worried, angry parents who saw their children failing in school saw decentralization as something different—and 'different' was better than the existing, failing school system.

There was a protracted dispute between those in the community who supported the Ocean Hill-Brownsville board and those supported UFT's argument that the teachers were illegally denied their rights.

135

A series of strikes ensued between September 9 and November 17, 1968. Many supporters of the local school board resorted to racial invective. Shanker was routinely branded a racist, and many African-Americans accused the UFT of being 'Jewish-dominated'.

Shanker was jailed for 15 days on February 3, 1969, for sanctioning the Ocean Hill-Brownsville strikes.

But the UFT prevailed. The teachers were re-instated and an agreement worked out reaffirming due process rights for New York City educators.

The Ocean-Hill Brownsville strike deeply affected the AFT. While the union formally recommitted itself to militancy, the AFT slowly began adopting a more moderate stand. Although AFT president David Selden would be arrested on February 23, 1970, during the Newark, New Jersey teachers' strike, becoming the third union president to go to jail, Selden's prison term would mark the last major AFT strike.

Many well-known Americans have been AFT members, including John Dewey, Albert Einstein, Hubert Humphrey, Pulitzer Prize-winning author Frank McCourt, Nobel Peace Prize winner Elie Wiesel, former Senate Majority Leader and Ambassador to Japan, Mike Mansfield, former Health and Human Services Secretary, Donna Shalala, and former United Nations Under-Secretary and Nobel Peace Prize, winner Ralph Bunche.

Mission Statement

The mission of the American Federation of Teachers, AFL-CIO, is to improve the lives of our members and their families; to give voice to their legitimate professional, economic and *social aspirations*; to strengthen the institutions in which we work; to improve the quality of the services we provide; to bring together all members to assist and support one another; and to *promote democracy, human rights and freedom in our union, in our nation and throughout the world.*   Author's note: This is full of progressive (communist) buzz words. They are italicized.

———————————————

We Are AFSCME

AFSCME is the nation's largest and fastest growing public services employees union with more than 1.6 million active and retired members. AFSCME's members provide the vital services that make America happen. We are nurses, corrections officers, child care providers, EMTs, sanitation workers and more. With members in hundreds of different occupations, AFSCME advocates for fairness in the workplace, excellence in public services and prosperity and opportunity for all working families.

AFSCME is a union comprised of a diverse group of people who share a common commitment to public service. For us, serving the public is not just a job, it's a calling. An important part of our mission is to advocate for the vital services that keep our families safe and make our communities strong. We also advocate for prosperity and opportunity for all of America's working families. We not only stand for fairness at the bargaining table — we fight for fairness in our communities and in the halls of government.

How AFSCME Works

AFSCME has approximately 3,400 local unions and 58 councils and affiliates in 46 states, the District of Columbia and Puerto Rico. Every local writes its own constitution, designs its own structure, elects its own officers and sets its own dues.

The International Union, based in Washington, DC, coordinates the union's actions on major national issues such as privatization, fair taxes and health care. The International also provides resources to councils and local unions for organizing, bargaining, political action and education, and administers members-only benefits. Every two years, delegates to AFSCME's International Convention decide on the union's basic policies. Every four years they elect the International Union's President, Secretary-Treasurer and 35 regional vice presidents.

This is a commentary written by the President of the AFSCME, Mr. Gerald W. McEntee. I chose this as the centerpiece of the union's credo since the preceding description seems to be very bland and fails to present the true character of the union. This piece must have been McEntee's final communique as President of the union.

The Good Fight

By Gerald W. McEntee
President, AFSCME

Sitting down to pen my last column for AFSCME WORKS, I am reminded of my father. A trash collector and union leader, he taught me that nothing mattered more than solidarity. He showed me that a good cause was always worth a good fight.

In the 1960s, I saw a good cause: 75,000 public service workers in Pennsylvania without a union. I led those workers in a good fight. We won the right to bargain collectively. We won fairness for workers.

Bigger Fights, Bigger Wins

But then as now, I knew that AFSCME always builds towards bigger fights, bigger wins.

The 1994 midterm elections were an all-out bloodbath. Republicans took control of the House and Senate, determined to gut Medicaid and Medicare. We fought the good fight. *We stopped the privatization of health care services that seniors and low-income families rely on.* And then we shook up the AFL-CIO, which desperately needed a sea change.

*In 2005, Pres. George W. Bush announced his **devastating plan to privatize Social Security**. Again, we fought the good fight. **We saved Social Security**. Out of that fight, with an eye towards building a stronger organization, our **Power To Win** plan was born.*

Though Power To Win gave us several years of powerful victories, we took a hit in the 2010 midterms. The right took back the House, 11 governorships and came after us. Like before, we made a plan — this time with our groundbreaking Battleground State Partnerships — and fought to victories in Wisconsin, Ohio, Florida and elsewhere

Author's note: All italicized emphasis is mine.

138

Tribute to the People

These defining moments in AFSCME's 75-year history are a tribute to the people who made them happen: people like you. You have revitalized this movement, this country. You have reaffirmed the meaning of my father's lesson on solidarity, and it has been a privilege to stand with you all these years.

On the eve of my retirement as president of our great union, I can look back with pride on all we've done to improve the lives of working Americans.

Our work is far from finished. Our accomplishments, our achievements are at risk. Corporate-backed politicians are trying to steal what we have fought for.

Even as we face our fiercest foes, I am not worried. You have proven that even in the face of the worst, you always give your best. Just as I knew AFSCME was meant for bigger, for better, back in the 1960s, I know that we are gearing up for the biggest wins we've seen in 2012 and beyond. Pulling together as one, I have no doubt that we will prevail.

Thank you, sisters and brothers, for your support, your commitment, your fight during the 56 years I have been a member of AFSCME and the 31 years I have had the honor of serving as president. You are just getting started. While leaders come and go, because of people like you, our union stays and stays and stays.

Paid for by the American Federation of State, County & Municipal Employees, AFSCME.org. Not authorized by any candidate or candidate's committee.